The Death of the Animal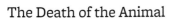

The Death of the Animal

A DIALOGUE

Paola Cavalieri

Foreword by Peter Singer

COLUMBIA

UNIVERSITY

PRESS

NEW YORK

Columbia University Press

Publishers Since 1893

New York   Chichester, West Sussex

Copyright © 2009 Columbia University Press

All rights reserved

Library of Congress Cataloging-in-Publication Data

Cavalieri, Paola, 1950-

The death of the animal : a dialogue / Paola Cavalieri ; foreword by Peter Singer.

    p.   cm.

Includes bibliographical references.

ISBN 978-0-231-14552-7 (cloth : alk. paper) — ISBN 978-0-231-51823-9 (electronic)

1. Animals (Philosophy). 2. Animal psychology. 3. Speciesism. 4. Intellect. I. Title.

B105.A55C37   2008

179'.3—dc22

2008015349

Contents

Acknowledgments

MY THANKS GO, first, to Franco Salanga, who has constantly provided essential criticism and support. Next, to Matthew Calarco, John Coetzee, Harlan Miller and Cary Wolfe for agreeing to participate in this enterprise, and to Peter Singer for writing the foreword. I owe a special debt to my editor, Wendy Lochner, for her insightful assistance, and to the two anonymous readers at Columbia University Press, whose comments substantially improved the book. Finally, I am grateful to Gregory Zucker for precious advice, and to Sue Donaldson for sharing with me her thoughts about the ethical issues addressed here.

Theo Glucksman, the characters in the dialogue, take it to be: should we grant to nonhuman animals a basic moral status equal to that of humans, or should we recognize gradations of moral status for humans?

If this argument were all that the book you are holding contained, it would be well worth reading, though those familiar with philosophical work about animals in recent decades would recognize that it draws on earlier work, including that of Cavalieri herself, in her tightly argued book, *The Animal Question*. What makes this volume original and particularly fascinating is that the dialogue about "The Death of the Animal" is itself the launching pad for a distinct and very lively debate about the nature of philosophy and the role that reason can play in ethics. That discussion gets started because, as the names of the dialogue's protagonists suggest, they come respectively from the analytic and the continental philosophical traditions. So, although the conversation proceeds with the clarity of analytic philosophy, it isn't long before Heidegger and Derrida are drawn into it. The differences between the two approaches to philosophy are brought into even sharper focus when the dialogue has concluded and other voices enter the discussion, in the roundtable that follows.

The ensuing set of exchanges between Cavalieri and Harlan Miller, on the one hand, and Matthew Calarco and Cary Wolfe, on the other, is one of those rare occasions in which people coming out of the analytic and the continental traditions actually meet in discussions on a specific subject and connect with each other's positions. The topic of how we should think about animals proves to be very well placed to get to the heart of some important differences about how we should do philosophy and how philosophy can relate to our everyday life. This discussion should be particularly enlightening—if I may use that term without showing too much bias—for those who grew up with the idea that the analytic tradition is conservative and part of the establishment, while the continental tradition, especially in its postmodern aspect, is more critical and more radical.

The discussion between two very distinct ways of doing philosophy is subsumed by an even larger challenge, posed by the novelist J. M. Coetzee, who in his pithy contributions to the book asks whether the dialogue between Warnock and Glucksman is not itself, in the heavy weight it gives to reasoned discussion, an instance of "perfectionism in practice." This leads Coetzee to suggest—as his character Elizabeth Costello has already suggested in the novel that bears her name—that it isn't ethical reasoning that leads us to form our views about animals and whether we should eat them, but something quite different, something more like a "conversion experience." Coetzee also refers to it as a "mute appeal" or, borrowing a term from Levinas, a "look." This experience comes first, and the philosophical argument is just a kind of rationalization for it.

In saying this, Coetzee sides with other skeptics, not all of them sympathetic to postmodernist critiques of the role of reason, about the role of argument in moral life.[1] He suggests that all the participants in this book are "where we are today"—that is, have a deep moral concern about the way animals are treated,

> not because once upon a time we read a book that convinced us that there was a flaw in the thinking underlying the way that we, collectively, treat nonhuman animals, but because in each of us there took place something like a conversion experience, which, being educated people who place a premium on rationality, we then proceeded to seek backing for in the writings of thinkers and philosophers.

But to this Harlan Miller says, in effect: "You don't speak for me." Miller changed his views about animals, he tells us, precisely because he found himself unable to refute philosophical arguments against the way we generally think about, and treat, animals. If Miller's and similar anecdotal accounts are right—and they are supported by one major sociological study of the modern animal movement[2]—then we have to credit ethical reasoning, of the kind exemplified in the dialogue with which this book begins, with greater efficacy than Coetzee and other skeptics are prepared to allow it.

There are, therefore, at least three major debates going on in this volume. There is the substantive ethical debate about whether perfectionism is defensible, and in particular, whether it can justifiably be used to bestow a higher moral status on human beings than on conscious nonhuman animals. There is the debate about whether to approach ethical issues using the tools of analytic philosophy, or instead to reflect on them in the manner of continental philosophers like Levinas and Derrida. But since such reflections are still a kind of philosophical reasoning, we can see Coetzee's challenge as raising a third issue: whether we should be reasoning or philosophizing about ethical issues at all—rather than, perhaps, writing novels that may open people to new ways of looking at the world in which we live.

To debate so many really major issues at such a high level in so short a book is a truly remarkable achievement. After reading the pages that follow, I am sure you will agree.

The Death of the Animal

The Death of the Animal

A Dialogue on Perfectionism

Prologue

A Greek island, a summer morning. Alexandra Warnock has fin-
ished her breakfast and is reading a book on a terrace, often stopping
to glance at the sea. She is joined by her friend, Theo Glucksman.

THEO: Hi, Alexandra—already at work?

ALEXANDRA: Hi Theo—not quite—oh, well, in a sense . . . I
am reflecting. And looking at something that reflects . . .

T: Do you mean the sea?

A: Yes. But please, Theo, sit down. It's a beautiful morning.

T: (*sitting by her side*) Thus, reflecting on what?

A: On ethics—to be a little formal: on the question of what is
right or what ought to be, so far as this depends upon our voluntary action. . . . Do you think that ethics can be perfected?

T: Well, in a sense, yes. We can develop more refined arguments or produce deeper thoughts. But in another sense, I think
not. Ethics is different from scientific disciplines, which are
marked by undeniable progress. Consider the relationship with
history. The development of most scientific disciplines has
made it implausible to appeal to their history as a source of guid-
ance and inspiration. The study of the heliocentric theory, for
example, is now in astronomy only of an erudite interest. Not so
with ethics, which focuses on values and norms.

A: So you think, for example, that it is normal—or better, correct—that contemporary philosophers keep sticking, for example, to the age-old virtue theory in ethics?

T: Yes—or that they get inspiration from, or defend, many views or attitudes of the great authors of the past.

A: Things are not so simple, I fear. Take the discipline that we call aesthetics. It certainly deals with values. But we don't think there has not been progress in aesthetics—at least progress that makes it possible to see some periods in the history of the discipline as somehow marked by forms of archaism. The same, I think, can hold for ethics as well.

T: An odd opinion, Alexandra. It is easy to see that ethics hasn't undergone any of those spectacular changes that we can immediately detect in other fields.

A: This is true—but it is also hardly surprising. Unlike science, ethical reflection is not concerned with understanding and transforming the world. And, differently from aesthetics, it has not to do with enlightened opinions about pleasant or even admirable things. Ethical reflection deals with basic, often dramatic clashes of interests. This cannot but make it more resistant to change. Those who might achieve change—those in power—are not interested in altering the theoretical status quo, and those who would be interested—the weak—are not able to do it.

T: Nonetheless, you think that there have actually been changes? Well, if you are referring, as I suggested, to the idea that ethics has undergone a process of refinement, so that the main views of the past need to be somewhat polished and restated before use . . .

A: Not quite. Stephen Toulmin once observed that it cannot matter to us exactly what, e.g., Socrates said—indeed, that what we are looking for in doing ethics must even be independent of whether or not Socrates even existed.[1] I agree. And, against this background of gaining distance from the revered legacy of our history, what I am referring to in particular is the idea that some points, or perspectives, of the past should be rejected as archaic, and should be gotten rid of in order to achieve a clearer idea of what is right or wrong.

T: Can you give me an example?

A: What I will give you is not an example—it is just the starting point of all my meditations . . .

T: . . . in front of the sea.

A: Not any sea—the Greek sea! Well, to be absolutely concise: what I am interested in are the questions of perfectionism, and of "the animal."

T: Absolutely concise, but not absolutely clear. What do you mean by perfectionism? And in which sense the animal?

A: The two notions are connected. With "perfectionism" I do not refer to the concept long used to express the idea that what counts ethically is the achievement of a particular sort of excellence in *human* life. I'm thinking instead of the more recent sense of a categorization of the moral status of individuals—that is, of conscious beings.

T: Moral status?

A: Forgive me, Theo—I sometimes forget that your continental tradition is so different! One's moral status is one's place in the moral community: how much does one count? To what degree are one's interests protected? As you can see, questions of moral status lie at the very core of ethics. And, to put it very simply, perfectionists hold that there is a hierarchy in moral status. They maintain that conscious beings, and their interests, deserve different consideration according to their level of possession of certain characteristics.

T: Thus, if I understand you well, perfectionism in this sense is a kind of gradualism—it accepts degrees in moral status. Some individuals matter more than some other individuals, and can be treated differently.

A: Exactly. But the term "perfectionism" is clearer because it better captures the idea that graduality in treatment is not based, for example, on random choice or on particular relations, but rather on the level of the presence of some favored elements. And what I am pondering is the idea that perfectionism is the legacy of atavisms that a perfected ethics can no longer accept.

T: One moment. You did not mention only perfectionism—you also mentioned the animal.

A: Yes, you are right. I also said that the two notions are connected. Actually, "the animal"—not the real, living, individual animals, such as the two seagulls you can see there, high in the sky, but a specific philosophical abstraction—has been, historically, an integral part of perfectionist views. "The animal" is what lies at the bottom of the perfectionist's hierarchy. It is, par excellence, the negative term of comparison.

T: On this, I must agree with you. In our philosophical tradition, the notion of animality seems to have been created just to serve the metaphysics of the primacy of human beings—to stress, by contrast, our superiority. In fact, it appears to play the role of a normative rather than a descriptive concept.[2]

A: You have perfectly grasped the point. One might say that the derogatory category of "the animal" is the metaphysical ground for and the existence condition of perfectionism. The notion of animality is the pole that sheds its negative light on whoever is to be derogated. Historically, the subjugation of human beings has been usually coupled with their "animalization"—think of slaves, women, the disabled, native peoples.... Even those who are on the side of the victims tend to accept this logic. "I am not an animal! I am a human being!" cries the Elephant Man. And a philosopher like Emmanuel Levinas, clearly accepting that to be anything other than "human" is ipso facto a degradation, defined his condition as a prisoner in a Nazi camp as subhuman, describing himself and his companions as being reduced to a "gang of apes" entrapped in their species....[3] Now, what if the time had come to erase such a negative notion from our mental landscape? Of course, it is not a question of rehabilitating nonhuman beings from an empirical point of view.

T: Something that, as far as I know, is currently being done in many scientific fields after centuries of complacent distortions.

A: Though, I would add, still with much difficulty, since even in this case the "data" tend to be interpreted under the influence of implicit metaphysical premises, which keep shaping their interpretation by an obstinate policing of the human/animal boundary.[4] The question I am referring to, however, is a more directly philosophical one. We should get rid of a metaphysical concept—the animal—and we should disentangle all the ethical notions or attitudes that, by overlapping and confusingly intertwining, keep perfectionism, together with "the animal," alive. But this is not a task for now, Theo. Let's go and have a swim in these clear waters.

T: I gladly accept, but only on condition that we continue our conversation.

A: Of course—tomorrow morning.

First Day

Alexandra Warnock is on the terrace, eyes closed. She starts when Theo Glucksman arrives. The Great Myths.

T: Alexandra—did I frighten you? Were you asleep?

A: Oh no, Theo . . . or perhaps yes. I was half-asleep.

T: I am sorry—I am a little late.

A: Don't worry, Theo—I wasn't going anywhere. I like staying here.

T: Along the way, I met Olga. Do you know her?

A: I think so. Is she tall and handsome, with long curly hair?

T: Yes. Olga is indeed beautiful. And a charming talker. She likes to tell tales. Today, she told me the intricate story of a cousin of hers, who has come back to Greece after a long absence. I somehow lost the sense of time.

A: It is incredible how stories and tales fascinate human beings. A great writer once stressed this point well, but now I can't remember his exact words. At any rate, this seems to be a good starting point for our conversation. . . .

T: In which sense?

A: If you remember, yesterday I hinted at the intertwined elements of our ethical discourse that support perfectionism, and, with it, the notion of "the animal."

T: Of course I remember.

A: Well, one of those elements is narratives. Human beings are not only charmed by stories in their individual lives. They cherish—indeed crave—general, collective stories as well. And they like to build great buildings on such stories. Narratives help them to make sense of the world and of their lives in it; they embody structures that offer answers to fundamental interpretive questions.

T: And is there anything wrong with that?

A: Of course not, as long as such narratives are not translated into normatively hierarchical frameworks. But the question is that, normally, the interpretations they embody are directly normative—while systematizing the world, they more or less implicitly set out obligations and taboos. And, even more importantly, they determine roles and questions of status.

T: Can you explain this a little better?

A: Think, for instance, of religious narratives. According to one of the most widespread among them, human beings were made by God in his own image, while nonhuman beings are mere creations. The latter are only a preparatory work, while the former are the apex of creation, directly molded by God. This is a story—how fascinating, I leave it to you to decide. But the fact is that such a story supports the normative implication that humans are superior beings, entitled to use nonhumans as they see fit. Do you remember—"have dominion over the fish of the sea, and over the fowl of the air, and over every living thing that moveth upon the earth"—?[5] Well, now, in secular ethics, we naturally discount the implications of narratives such as this. Religious people, we think, can have their beliefs, but these beliefs cannot normatively influence an acceptable universal ethics. The problem is, however—

т: I think I am starting to understand what you're driving at.

а: That is to say?

т: You are going to say that there is a philosophical counterpart of such religious narratives.

а: Exactly—and that we do not behave in the same way when the normative implications of philosophical narratives are concerned.

т: I agree with you on the first point. If I remember well, Friedrich Nietzsche once noticed that, because philosophers often philosophized in traditional religious habits, or at least under the old inherited power of the same "metaphysical need," they arrived at dogmas that greatly resembled religious doctrines.[6] It is indisputable that there is a philosophical counterpart of religious narratives. Mainstream Western philosophers have been traditionally interested in constructing large-scale, superscientific explanations of things, typically characterized by a claim to some form of transcendent and universal truth. But what about normativity?

а: The point is, Theo, that, along the lines of the religious tradition of which such philosophical narratives are the theoretical heirs, ethics is swallowed up into the huge general systems built to explain the universe. In other words, general standards of status and norms for conduct are directly derived from these systems.

т: For example?

а: Oh, the examples are so many that it is difficult to choose. But perhaps the case of Martin Heidegger is particularly telling, as he was so explicit on this point. According to Heidegger, the basic philosophical question is, why is there anything at all, rather than nothing?[7] In the face of such a grand question, what role can ethics play? A very minor and dependent one, we might guess. And in fact Heidegger, who did not personally devote much attention to the question, when pressed to formulate his views about it, claimed that ethics should reflect "man's" place, and that such a thinking of man's original element, though being in itself original ethics, is to begin with not ethics at all, but rather ontology.[8] Nothing could illustrate more clearly how a possible code concerning both how to live and how individuals should be treated might be directly derived from a philosophical myth.

т: "Myth"? Isn't the word somehow too strong?

A: Why strong? The word "myth"—which, as you know, in Greek means simply a "relating," "a telling word"—is currently used in the sense of a more or less sacred story that can convey a lot of meaning but resides outside the disjunction true or false. "Myth" is the term we use to define the great metaphors that Plato—the last sage before the beginning of systematic philosophy, the most imaginative of ancient authors—used to illustrate his interpretations of the world. But "myth" is a term we might also use for the interpretations themselves—and not only in the case of Plato.

т: What you mean is that such interpretations are undemonstrable?

A: Yes, you can put it like that. And the same holds in the case of the interpretations offered by Aristotle, or Thomas Aquinas, or Leibniz, or Hegel—the list is quite long. For what did these remarkable thinkers do but offer great superscientific constructions residing beyond any possible verification, falsification, or simply rational challenge? How can we prove or disprove the idea that the ultimate reality is substance, or that there is any natural divine law, or that we live in the best possible world, or that history manifests the realization of the absolute spirit?

т: Or that language is the House of Being, just to go back to Heidegger.[9]

A: That is one of my preferred quotations. . . . Of course, we can find all or some of these views illuminating—we can gloss and discuss them, as so many philosophers do—but undoubtedly their nature is such that none of them can aspire to receive a general and uncontroversial rational assent. How can one say what might justify a belief in this field? Though we know how to correct our beliefs on physical objects, we have no idea regarding how to correct metaphysical beliefs on the ultimate nature of things. But . . . Theo, are you listening to me?

т: Oh, sorry, Alexandra—I was just reflecting. . . .

A: In the meantime, do you want some orange juice? It's becoming rather hot today.

T: Yes, please. How nice is it to drink when one is thirsty. . . . Oh, well, I was thinking that. I mean, is it necessary to attack in a specific way all these, let's say, ontological views, when you could have appealed, more generally, to the is/ought question? In other words, why do you put so much stress on the fact that these views are, as you say, undemonstrable, when you probably subscribe to Hume's logical point that it is always unwarranted to draw normative conclusions from descriptive premises?[10] You might as well criticize any ethical approach based on scientific, demonstrable facts.

A: My dear Theo, you are certainly right—but only in a sense. Of course, I do not accept a direct derivation of values from scientific facts—such as, for example, one can find in some views in environmental ethics.

T: For example?

A: Well, for example those that locate the ultimate value in the biotic community and determine the moral status of beings on the basis of their contribution, to borrow the famous words of conservationist Aldo Leopold, to the "integrity, stability, and beauty" of the whole.[11] Clearly, by using scientific interpretations of the world as guides for philosophical conclusions, such views violate Hume's law. However, one must keep the distinctions clear. Unlike metaphysics, science can play a role in discussions of moral status. For one can—indeed, must—point to relevant empirical "data" (however deconstructed this notion may be) to substantiate specific moral claims—as when one stresses evidence of consciousness, or of particular psychological mechanisms, in this or that entity.

T: Also, on a different level, it seems to me that science can help us to better understand the phenomenon of morality, looking for its pretheoretical roots.

A: A good observation. Actually, sociobiological and ethological inquiries on the development of moral codes and virtues in social animals can reframe some of our questions and redirect some of our answers. There is room for argument and discussion here. The metaphysical views we mentioned, on the other hand, are quite another thing. They are systems of statements that are only apparently related as premises and conclusions. As Rudolf Carnap once put it, they do not assert anything, but merely express something.[12] Both they and their use are archaic—a unquestioned legacy of the past.

T: That they are archaic in the sense of being dogmatic—of being, in other words, characterized by authoritative and often unconnected assertions of unproved principles or facts—one cannot deny. But can you be clearer about the question of their use?

A: The fact is that their idiosyncratic descriptions of the world tend to be naturally, though sometimes almost unnoticeably, translated into forms of perfectionism—that is, into hierarchies in moral status—due to the ancestral element of all-inclusivity they inherit from religion. As we have seen, traditionally, religious views are overall, integrated explanations of things already embodying normative aspects—their "is" already embodies an "ought." The same holds for the ontological views in question. For in their case too ethics merely plays an ancillary role—that of calling for the realization of values that already exist within "being" and issue from it.

T: But in a sense, this is normal, Alexandra. If you accept a philosophical interpretation of the world, you are guided and motivated by its insights. Just to mention an author who did have an interest, albeit minor, in the animal question, Arthur Schopenhauer: if one is convinced by his "will metaphysics," and by the theory of morals issuing from it, one will naturally embrace compassion, even toward nonhumans.[13] Perhaps one will also embrace self-renunciation.

A: I see your point, Theo. Actually, I should have been clearer about a fundamental issue. The fact is that ethics has as its object two sorts of theory of conduct. One is morality in the broad sense—an all-inclusive theory of conduct, which includes precepts about the good life, the character traits to be fostered, the values to be pursued. The other is morality in the narrow sense—a system of constraints on conduct, usually expressed in terms of negative duties, whose task is to protect the interests of others—e.g., do not harm, do not confine, do not kill. Questions of moral status—the questions in which we are now interested—concern morality in the narrow sense. If, in the case of broad morality, the demand to pursue a specific conception of the good life may leave room for the arbitrariness of specific worldviews, when it comes to defining toward whom one should restrict one's conduct, the requirement for justification is the most stringent. Accordingly, appeals to undemonstrable metaphysical claims are unacceptable.

T: So you mean that were I, say, a follower of Schopenhauer I might personally conform to his idea of a central role for compassion in ethics, but I would be barred from the attempt to socially implement his views concerning the treatment of individuals.... Well, if I think, for example, of his infamous claims about the inferiority of women, it is certainly not difficult for me to agree with you![14] But of course your point is not substantive but formal. It refers to the way ideas and rules are produced, not to their content.

A: Exactly so. And the adjective "social" that you employed is perfectly chosen, Theo. Indeed, narrow morality can be also called "social morality," because it is not about diversity of kinds of life but about uniformity of practices.[15] Its content pertains to the realm of the right, not to that of the good—to the domain of the obligatory, not of the supererogatory.

T: Your previous reference to Schopenhauer was enlightening. Can you offer a few other concrete illustrations? The argument is dense, the day is hot....

A: You are right, Theo. And I was just about to give you some more examples. Imagine that you are a "barbarian" in an Aristotelian world. You would be seen as an inferior being since according to Aristotle there must exist a union of natural rulers and subjects, and those who can "foresee by the exercise of mind"—of course, Greek men—are by nature intended to be masters, while those who can work with their body—all non-Greeks—are subjects, and by nature slaves.[16] Or imagine that you are a woman in a moral context dominated by Aquinas's thought. Would you accept being considered a less valuable being than a man, because according to Aquinas the active force in the male seed tends to the production of a perfect likeness in the masculine sex, while the production of women comes from a defect in the active force and, consequently, women are characterized by a defect in the reason?[17] Finally—

T: Sorry to interrupt you, Alexandra, but it strikes me that there was at least a point of agreement between authors so distant as Aquinas and Schopenhauer...

A: And many, many other authors. A philosopher once wrote that, when it comes to women, admirable theorists lose all sense of what their general style of thinking demands and simply recite clichés.[18] Indeed, to be precise, she referred not only to the case of women but also to the case of animals. So, a final example regarding members of species other than our own. Imagine that you are a nonhuman animal. From a Heideggerian point of view, you could be lightheartedly killed, as you would not die, but merely perish. And this because, for Heidegger, "man" is not just a living thing possessing language, but rather lives within language, which is the place for Being, while nonhumans, lacking language, are "poor-in-world" and perennially "captured."[19]

T: Quite clear now, Alexandra, quite clear. An acceptable narrow morality should get rid of these myths, no matter how great they may be. Of course, individuals cannot be at the mercy of idiosyncratic metaphysical hierarchies . . .

A: . . . and the value of their lives and interests cannot be degraded or discounted on the basis of arbitrary perfectionist interpretations of the universe. While ethics as a discipline is still burdened by a past in which it hadn't yet attained its autonomy, everyday morality is starting to understand this. But that is for tomorrow, I daresay.

T: Yes, Alexandra. But tomorrow I have problems in the early morning—I can join you only around noon. Is that all right with you?

A: It is perfect, Theo!

T: But why are you smiling?

A: I'll tell you tomorrow. Now, what about refreshing our minds with a dive into the sea?

Second Day

The sun is high in the sky, and the little bay is still and silent. Theo enters the terrace, which is empty. While he perches on the parapet, looking at the sea, Alexandra joins him. Masters and Slaves.

A: Hi, Theo. A wonderful time, isn't it?

T: Yes, Alexandra.

A: We feel the magic of such moments. It's the Great Noon.

T: Are you thinking of Friedrich Nietzsche? But he loved the mountains.

A: Not only the mountains, Theo. He loved the sea too. But you guessed what I referred to. And that is why I was smiling yesterday. Please, sit down here, in the shade.

T: You smiled because . . .

A: . . . because some—though not I myself—might consider our argument for today very Nietzschean, revolving as it does around masters and slaves.[20]

T: Why not yourself?

A: Well, because Nietzsche's distinction between masters and slaves did not focus, at least explicitly, on levels of moral status, but rather on types of moralities. And maybe also because I hold that Nietzsche's thinking harbored quite different, perhaps opposite, positions as well. . . . However, to go back to the further brick added to the wall of perfectionism I wanted to consider—

T: I'd say that, in philosophy, when one thinks of slavery, the first name that comes to mind is Aristotle.

A: Quite so, Theo. And it is indeed from Aristotle that we shall start. In concluding a survey of what he calls the misfortunes of virtue, Jerome Schneewind observes that the Aristotelian theory of virtue was suited to a society in which there was a recognized class of superior citizens, whose judgment on moral issues would be accepted without question. Virtue ethics sees character at the core of morality, and supposes that the central moral question is not, what ought I to do? but, what sort of individual am I to be? And Schneewind stresses that in its first, Aristotelian formulation, virtue theory was clearly concerned only with "superior" individuals—if not heroes, at least male, free members of a preferred ethnic group—do you remember the comment on "barbarians"?[21]

T: Of course I do.

A: Now, Aristotle's blessed few dominated a scene crowded with inferiors—women, slaves, children, strangers—whose virtue resided in being at their service. To these blessed few were reserved the practice of the "golden mean" in dealing with their attitudes, the active life of the political community, and the supreme activity of theoretical contemplation. Even more than general criteria, it was their wisdom or *phronesis* that decided moral dilemmas.

T: Put like that, it seems that this kind of virtue ethics is not able to do at least one of the things we currently ask from morality—that is, to handle serious disagreements *among equals*.

A: You got directly to the point, Theo.

T: Yes, but may I add that this is no longer the case with later, and especially contemporary, versions of virtue theory? Maybe with some difficulty, but many authors have disposed of this antiegalitarianism.

A: Perhaps you are right, Theo, though I am not so sure.... At any rate, even if such first-level antiegalitarism might be eliminated from virtue ethics, there exists a second-level antiegalitarianism that cuts deeper in the theory, because it has to do with its very structure.

T: A second-level antiegalitarianism? What do you mean?

A: A rather simple thing. By seeing morality as a set of orientations for developing forms of excellence and for giving meaning to one's life, virtue ethics gives center stage to moral agents, that is, to those beings whose *behavior* can be subject to moral evaluation. Accordingly, it dismisses or discounts mere moral patients, that is, those beings whose *treatment* may be subject to moral evaluation.

T: Let's make this point clear, Alexandra, before proceeding. If I understand well, a moral agent is a being who can reflect morally on how to act, and who can be held accountable for her actions.

A: Perfect. And a moral patient is a being who is morally considerable in itself. Moral patients are the beings who should be taken into account when deciding how to act—the beings whose interests deserve direct protection.

T: In other words, they are the "others" of the golden rule.

A: Right. And of course moral agents too are moral patients, when they are, so to speak, at the recipient end of the action. That's why I just spoke of mere moral patients, though the shorter "moral patients" is normally used to cover both the narrower and the wider sense.

T: All right, thanks—now you can resume the argument.

A: Well, what I was saying is that what virtue theory does—especially when, through a sort of "eliminatism," it aims at doing all the work of ethics—is to confine attention to a special subclass of the beings that can be affected by the agent's action. Among the many beings endowed with interests that can be thwarted, virtue ethics chooses to give protection—or special protection—only to those that have some favored characteristics, thus building an antiegalitarian moral community.

T: You mean that some beings that are morally considerable—moral patients—are structurally discounted with respect to other morally considerable beings—that is, moral agents? Is this the second-level antiegalitarianism you contrast to the first-level one of the blessed few?

A: Yes, and—

T: No, wait a moment . . . I am thinking of Kant. There is perhaps in his approach an unwitting connection between the first and the second level. In discussing the original social contract, Kant includes among the principles that must govern the "condition of right" the independence of each member of the commonwealth as a citizen. With this, he means that (adult, male) individuals can have a right to vote on specific laws only if they are masters of themselves, i.e., are not someone else's servants or employees.[22] It seems to me that here the Kantian notion of moral autonomy as a ground for superior moral status is directly translated into the notion of economic autonomy as a ground for superior political status. All this somehow echoes the antiegalitarian social bent of the initial form of virtue ethics.

A: I never noticed that, Theo. In a sense, it is quite revealing.

T: But I interrupted you. You were saying that—

A: That, as far as the deep structure of virtue ethics is concerned, the building of an antiegalitarian moral community can happen in several different ways. It can occur by a mere act of omission—by simply letting moral patients glide unnoticed into the shadows and be forgotten within the landscape of the pursuit of excellence—or by the overt defense of a hierarchy in levels of moral status. In all cases, however, perfectionism creeps in as a focus on the quintessential form of the moral agent, able to understand and apply principles and norms. For it is clear that, in order to reflect morally on how to act, one should obviously possess some demanding cognitive elements.

T: Are you referring to the favored elements you hinted at when we started our conversation? I'm glad that we are getting to this point.

A: Actually, you have already been confronted with them, though in an indirect way. While many have been the characteristics required for admission into the circle of moral agents—humans are imaginative beings!—no doubt the most commonly mentioned are three: self-consciousness, rationality, and conceptual-linguistic abilities. Doesn't this list have a familiar ring to it?

T: In a general sense, the list is indeed quite familiar. The characteristics you refer to are certainly deeply cherished in our philosophical tradition. But more particularly?

A: More particularly, wasn't a form of self-consciousness what Aristotle appealed to in defining the masters as contrasted to the slaves? Wasn't reason what Aquinas employed to draw the line between woman and man? And finally, wasn't language what carried so much weight with Heidegger? You can clearly see here a first instance of the overlapping between various ethical attitudes I mentioned at the beginning. Such overlapping grants surreptitious plausibility to each of them, insofar as the claims of the one draw acceptability from the analogous claims of the other. We see here a sort of redundancy effect.

T: Can you be clearer?

A: Redundancy occurs when there is "more than the minimum." Here, the claims about the moral relevance of the favored characteristics, being apparently supported by various views, offer more than the minimum justification. Redundancy of information affords obvious advantages to the defenders of a view, for it helps to confirm expectations and renders it more difficult to master complex problems. This makes it necessary to disentangle and analytically examine the different elements before it becomes possible to challenge them. But are you tired, Theo?

T: Tired? Not at all. I am getting more and more intrigued. But what about you?

A: Not tired either—perhaps a little thirsty. Let me get something fresh. . . .

Alexandra disappears into the shadowy room. Theo gets up and takes a few steps on the terrace. Alexandra comes back carrying a tray with a carafe. She pours the beverage and offers a glass to Theo.

T: Alexandra, your interest is not merely theoretical, correct? You have practical goals.

A: Correct, Theo.

T: Well, let's sit down again, and please go on. What, then, about the three favored cognitive characteristics you mentioned?

A: Before proceeding, there is a question we should briefly touch upon. When philosophers construe these abilities, they usually do it in a dogmatic, unquestioning way. In particular, self-consciousness, rationality, and conceptual-linguistic capacities are defined in a categoric manner, which totally overlooks their actual multidimensional and gradational nature.

T: Are you suggesting that philosophers tend to employ ideological constructions rather than empirically verified phenomena?

A: Exactly, Theo. It is partly a problem of mistrust for and lack of familiarity with science, and partly the old problem of policing the boundary. And the odd thing is that their interpretations are so rigid as to de facto exclude many members of our species. This is something that the Neoplatonist philosopher Porphyry already stressed in the context of his case for philosophical vegetarianism, when he claimed that, according to the criteria of some philosophers, only a small minority of human beings could be considered rational, boldly adding that it is apparent that "many of our own species live from sense alone, but do not possess intellect and reason."[23] However, for the sake of argument, let's set this problem aside, in order to continue our survey.

T: Well, it seems to me that the favored set of abilities cannot bring much grist to the mill of perfectionism when inserted in metaphysical—let alone religious—contexts. What, then, about the possible justifications for a perfectionist stress on these very abilities within the context of virtue ethics?

A: I'd say that, if one looks at the history of moral philosophy, the justifications appear to cluster, though not always explicitly, around a key idea. The idea is that moral agents are the existence condition of morality. If moral agents did not exist—so the argument goes—there could be no ethical norms. As a consequence, ethics is an internal affair of moral agents.

T: Apparently plausible.

A: Yes, apparently plausible—but actually based on a conceptual confusion. For the conclusion of the argument is reached merely by the shift from the idea that only moral agents can be morally responsible to the idea that only what is done to moral agents has moral weight.

T: You mean that—

A: —that one thing is the *how*, that is, the possibility of morality, and another is the *what*, that is, the object—or function—of morality.[24] To acknowledge that moral agents make morality possible does not mean to make them the only moral patients.

T: And yet, this is a quite ingrained and widespread view.

A: So ingrained and widespread that a name has been coined for it— the "agent-patient parity principle." But the idea that the class of moral patients coincides with the class of moral agents, far from being a self-evident ground for justification, stands in need of justification. And that we do not think such justification is easily found is shown by the fact that everyday morality rejects the idea that children or intellectually disabled individuals, who are unable to abide by ethical norms, are excluded from the moral community.

T: Is this one of the instances of the superiority of everyday morality over ethics as a discipline that you hinted at yesterday?

A: Yes, Theo. It is indeed curious how long the agent-patient parity principle has dominated Western ethics, and how seriously it is still taken today from a philosophical point of view. Perhaps, then, we should inspect it more closely. . . . Thus, why should we grant exclusive—or, in a softened version, superior—moral value to moral agents?

T: Well, perhaps because, somehow following Socrates, we think that an examined—or, better, a morally responsible—life is better than the opposite?

A: I'm sorry, Theo, but though you are in good company in giving such an answer—which seems to be taken for granted by quite a few thinkers—what we face here is another conceptual confusion. Indeed, this argument involves a category mistake. For it is one thing to say that an individual who can act morally, and chooses to do so, is better than another individual who can act morally, but doesn't choose to do so—

T: —and another thing to say that an individual who can act morally is better than an individual who cannot act morally! I understand what you mean. I can think I am better than, say, a rapist who knowingly disregards the interests of his victim; but I cannot therefore conclude that I am better than a small child who impulsively hits her brother out of jealousy. . . . In the former case the comparison is between different actualizations of the same capacities, and in the latter it is between different capacities.

A: Exactly so, Theo. Thus, we can exclude the "Socratic" answer as based, to say the least, on a misunderstanding. If, on the other hand, one claims, as we have mentioned, that moral agents matter more because they are necessary if morality is to exist at all, without any further consideration of the point of morality, it seems that the only point of morality is: for morality itself to be able to exist.

T: An odd view, I must admit.

A: And one that could be defended only within the framework of an idiosyncratic worldview, granting morality a peculiar sort of solipsistic value. There is, however, a different reply to our question—one that can indeed be put in universal terms. Moral agents count for more, it can be claimed, because the introduction into the moral community can be justified by means of some sort of agreement. Since in order to abide by the agreement one must be a moral agent, the agreement will include only moral agents, who will thus turn out to be the only moral patients.

T: Thus, if I understand well, on this view moral norms would be the norms with which rational and self-interested individuals would agree to comply on condition that others agreed to do so as well. In other words, my compliance with the norms is the fair price I pay to secure your compliance. . . . It is not hard to detect behind this the elements of what have come to be known as contract theories.

A: You are perfectly right, Theo. But at this point, we should perhaps pause a little. For our line of reasoning has led us to a surprising conclusion—it has suggested a relationship between two quite separate, and often diverging, approaches to ethics. For virtue theory and contract theory have actually been, and still are, two serious contenders within the discipline—the former focusing on individual responsibility and on flexibility of behavior, the latter on strict general principles covering social morality.

T: And yet, it seems that there are common elements lying deep within them. . . .

A: Indeed. First, unlike other models that, like utilitarianism and some rights theories, start from the, so to speak, morally relevant passive side of individuals, focusing on interests or on preferences, virtue ethics and contractarianism start from the morally relevant active side of individuals, insofar as they concentrate on moral attitudes or agency. Second, though perhaps less evidently, both approaches give prominent place to the element of self-interest—contractarianism by a direct appeal to it, and virtue ethics by the moral pursuit of an ideal form of life that is also the prudential pursuit of a meaningful, "good" life.

T: In this light, I think I must reframe my previous question about the possible justifications for a perfectionist stress on the favored set of characteristics. And the new question seems to be: does the contractarian approach offer any sound theoretical support for virtue ethics', as well as for its own, stress on moral agents?

A: A correct framing, Theo, I daresay. And to try to answer this question, we can consider the version of contractarianism that appeals to the doctrine of your cherished Immanuel Kant—a doctrine in which, by the way, we do find side by side both the idea of a social contract and an ethics of virtue. Contractarianism of Kantian descent, which has been made famous by John Rawls's theory of justice, is usually defined as "impartial contractarianism." That moral demands are impartial is, of course, acknowledged by most moral theories. For its part, impartial contractarianism—along the lines of Kant's suggestion that the rightful social contract does not exist as a fact, but is a regulative idea of reason[25]—sees (the most important sphere of) morality as the result of a hypothetical contract between rational agents. In other words, it tries to justify a system of moral principles by showing that agents would agree on them in a specified hypothetical circumstance—under a "veil of ignorance" that would prevent them from knowing their individual plight in society.[26]

T: If I understand you, then, on this view it is hypothetical choice, under hypothetical circumstances, that sets the standard for moral legitimacy, because such a choice embodies impartiality.

A: Perfect. The basic idea is that, though self-interested, the agents would opt for an impartial protection and distribution of goods insofar as they would aim at granting themselves fair treatment in case they ended up the worse-off in the actual world.

T: "There but for the grace of God go I" . . .

A: Well, more or less.

T: Thus, the device of—of the veil of ignorance seems to prevent any moral sanctioning of concrete bargaining power.

A: It seems, but it doesn't. For a sinister element that has been eliminated at the level of the agreement between the parties is reintroduced at the level of admission to the discussion of the agreement. It is the idea of reciprocity.

T: Reciprocity a sinister idea? That's curious—why do you say so?

A: Indeed, Theo, whenever I express such a judgment, I must face scandalized objections. And I concede there is a point in them—but only if they are strictly qualified.

T: That is to say?

A: As the philosopher James Rachels puts it, the requirement of reciprocity does contain the germ of a plausible idea. If an individual is capable of acting considerately of your interests, and refuses to do so, then you may be released from any similar obligation you might have toward her.[27] But this is a very specific case, and one in which impartialism is not in question. In fact, reciprocity has little to do with impartialism. It replaces the golden rule "treat others as you would have them treat you" with what we might call the silver rule, "treat others as they would treat you."[28]

T: Actually, Schopenhauer once said something along these lines. . . . Indeed, if I remember well, he put it more bluntly, as he suggested that, under the condition of reciprocity, egoism cunningly acquiesces in a compromise.[29]

A: Not only Schopenhauer was so clear, Theo, but Friedrich Nietzsche was as well. He claimed without hesitation that justice or fairness, being based on reciprocity and exchange between roughly equal parties, is clearly connected with egoism—or, to quote his exact words, that it "naturally goes back to the viewpoint of an insightful self-preservation."[30]

T: This is rather convincing.

A: And you can see this point more clearly if you consider what reciprocity implies in conditions of serious imbalances in power. It is difficult to understand how being impartial is compatible with the fact of completely ignoring the interests of those who are unable to reciprocate. But rational contractors turn out to be entitled to do just this, since they gain no advantage from accepting principles that offer guarantees to individuals who are unable to give any guarantee in return.

T: How, then, can an "impartialist" perspective make room for this notion?

A: As far as Rawls is concerned, the key seems to lie in the fact that, when considering who is a party to the hypothetical contract, his perspective, following David Hume's account of the circumstances of justice, keeps inserting relative equality within the normal conditions under which social cooperation is both possible and necessary.[31] True, such relative equality does not refer to actual threatening power; it refers instead to moral personality, that is, to the fact of being a moral agent. But while the contract is hypothetical, the requirement of moral agency is an actual one. The impartial choice of principles under an ideal circumstance is limited to the parties that are moral agents *in real life*. Rawls himself is quite clear on this—he states that, by giving justice to those who can give justice in return, the principle of reciprocity is fulfilled at the highest level.

T: You mentioned David Hume, Alexandra. I must say that today is a day of strange associations. In the first place, you point to a connection between virtue theory and contractarianism. Then you point to a connection between Kant's ethics and Hume's ethics. . . .

A: Does this suggest to you that I am going wild?

T: Oh no, Alexandra. What it does suggest to me is that, all considered, the number of main ideas in our past ethical reflection is not as large as we might have thought! But let's return to impartial contractarianism and to the unsoundness of its focus on the demanding cognitive skills required for moral agency.

A: Well, though we are still far from crude mutual-advantage contractarianism of Hobbesian descent, where harm to innocent individuals lacking any threatening power can be rendered just by their mere inability to organize effective resistance, when all the dust has settled, here too it is just the weak and infirm who receive less moral protection. This, as has been observed, is a "mockery" of the idea of morality.[32] For justice is normally thought of not as ceasing to be relevant in conditions of extreme inequality in power, but rather as being especially relevant in such conditions.

T: And is it fair to say that, as a consequence of the stress on reciprocity, not only nonhuman animals but also nonparadigmatic—that is, intellectually disabled—human beings turn out to be excluded from the higher moral sphere?

A: It is fair, if one rejects the introduction of slippery slope arguments and appeals to special relationships.

T: And why should one reject them?

A: Well, slippery slope arguments would simply duplicate the reference to self-interest we have just criticized in discussing the very notion of reciprocity. In this context, the idea that we should not take steps that might lead to further steps at the end of which there is something we want to avoid would be translated into the idea that we should not exclude nonparadigmatic humans from the higher moral sphere because of the risk that such a step might in the long run lead to our own exclusion! As for appeals to special relationships, they are the Trojan horse of any possible discrimination—think only of the resort to such appeals in defense of preference for the members of one's tribe, or race, or . . .

T: I understand. Thus, it seems we can conclude that contract theory's—and virtue theory's!—preferential focus on moral agents is unwarranted.

A: Yes, Theo. The moral agent—the self-conscious, rational, and linguistically able individual—has no special claim as moral patient.

T: In other words, there is no place for a perfectionist distinction between masters and slaves in our contemporary egalitarian morality.

A: No place, luckily. Nor is there any place for the perfectionist distinction between the category of "man"—please notice the gender!—and the category of "the animal." In a sense, the continued philosophical defense of such hierarchical approaches can be regarded as a "living fossil" in the field of ideas.

T: I suppose we have reached the end of the argument for today . . . and I suppose I shall be going now. (*He stands up.*) But it is difficult to extricate myself abruptly from all this. I'm glad I have to walk a little to get back home. . . . Alexandra, what about meeting in the afternoon, tomorrow?

A: When all lights grow quieter? It's perfect. See you tomorrow, Theo.

Third Day

Alexandra and Theo enter the terrace together. Their hair is wet, and they are laughing. They drop onto the chairs. The Magic of Intrinsic Value.

T: We shall remember these days, Alexandra.

A: Definitely. But shall you keep in mind our conclusions too, and act upon them?

T: You never give up, Alexandra.

A: No, of course. Isn't the aim of ethics practical? Doesn't ethics deal with the rational pursuit of the goal of bettering the lot of vulnerable beings?

T: Though I personally agree with you, not all philosophers would subscribe to this. Possibly the majority wouldn't.

A: Perhaps not, if you think of the authors who are still devoted to creating the great myths. However—

T: However?

A: I was about to say that in other areas the situation is radically different, but probably you are more nearly right than I thought. . . . Before the turn marked by the project of grounding ethics in its own sphere of reason, the rise of analytic philosophy was indeed accompanied by the idea that ethics has no goals and can allow only a limited, collateral role for rational argument.

T: Are you referring to the logical positivists' view that reason's only verifiable statements are either logical or empirical, and that, since moral statements fall outside both of these categories, moral statements are meaningless?

A: Exactly, Theo—I am just referring to this impoverished approach to reason, and to the attendant claim that ethical propositions are nothing more than the expression, or stating, of preferences and attitudes—be they personal or collective. . . .[33] Thus, in the analytic tradition as well one can find authors who have not attained the conception of ethics I referred to.

T: A good instance, it seems to me, is Ludwig Wittgenstein in his famous lecture on ethics.

A: Perfect, Theo, a perfect example, and well in tune with the last point I wanted to touch upon.

T: Namely?

A: Our final target is the notion of intrinsic value—a notion often put to use, or at least implicitly appealed to, within defenses of perfectionist accounts of moral status. Intrinsic value is central to Wittgenstein's lecture. Curiously enough, in this text by one of the fathers of analytic philosophy, there is something strongly reminiscent of the position of so distant an author as Heidegger. If you remember, speaking of the attempt to fix his mind on what he means by ethical value, Wittgenstein states that he believes the best way of describing such an experience is to say that when he has it he wonders at the existence of the world.[34]

T: Of course I remember. And he adds that he is inclined to use such phrases as "how extraordinary that anything should exist."

A: Wonderful, Theo—you are always so precise!

T: And then, after commenting that Ethics (with a capital e), if it is anything, is supernatural, while our words only express facts, he concludes that such experience seems to him to have in some sense an intrinsic, absolute value, and that no description that he can think of would do to describe what he means by such value. . . .

A: Perfect. It is exactly this conclusion that I wanted to stress. Apart from the fact that, were ethics, contrary to what I suggested, that sort of supernatural thing Wittgenstein wants it to be, there would be precious little we could do to counteract both active malevolence and selfishness in our daily life, the relevant point is that it appears here most clearly an essential aspect of the notion of intrinsic value. It is the religious—indeed, supernatural—halo that surrounds it. And one thing is immediately apparent: the reverence and awe that the notion may inspire, while perhaps summoning acceptance and compliance, are certainly far from fostering analysis and argument.

T: The analysis and argument that you are just about to offer?

A: You are teasing me, Theo. . . . But in fact, the problem is just this— to examine more closely what it can mean to say of something that it has intrinsic value. And of course I am not the first one to do this. So we can borrow from what an American philosopher, Ben Bradley, has suggested.[35] For Bradley, the answer to our question is twofold. On one side, to say of something that it has intrinsic value means to affirm that the value of the entity is not bestowed from outside, but is an integral part of the thing itself; on the other, it means instead that the entity can never be used merely as a means.

T: Quite interesting.

A: And, according to Bradley, this twofold answer points to the existence of two conceptions of intrinsic value, distinguishable by their different theoretical roles. If one is interested in answering certain questions in an overall theory of value, one is supposed to talk about a certain notion of intrinsic value—like the one defended by G. E. Moore—that is connected with the idea that what has intrinsic value makes the world a better place just by being around.[36] If one is instead interested in determining the moral status of individuals and the ways they can be treated, one is supposed to refer to another notion of intrinsic value, traditionally traced to Immanuel Kant, which is connected with the idea that having intrinsic value means to be an end in itself.

T: And which one of the two conceptions seems to you sounder?

A: The fact is, Theo, that I find such a distinction, as you say, interesting—but not satisfying. To see why, let us start directly from the Kantian notion of end in itself. How does Kant justify the attribution of this kind of intrinsic—or "absolute"—value?

T: Well, if I recall correctly, while defending the principle that rational nature exists as an end in itself, Kant offers an alleged proof of its validity. In brief: since the human being necessarily thinks of his own existence as an end in itself, and since every other rational being thinks of his existence in the same way, it is an objective principle that rational nature exists as an end in itself.[37]

A: Just so. And it seems to me clear that, as a logical proof, the argument is hardly satisfying. For if the two premises are descriptive statements, the conclusion, which is a normative statement, is unwarranted. And if, on the other hand, the two premises are normative statements, in the sense that they refer to what rationality imposes as duty, the argument, far from offering a demonstration, becomes circular. From a heuristic point of view, however, Kant's suggested proof is interesting. For in this perspective Kantian intrinsic or absolute value, far from having an objective foundation, seems to take shape as the value that some individuals grant to themselves beyond, and in opposition to, any value they might have for others. It becomes, therefore, an attribute of subjectivity—the end in itself becomes end for itself. Apparently, we are here on an unusual track.

т: But only apparently?

a: Yes, because if Kantian intrinsic value can be seen as a sort of external projection—a hypostatization—of the value that the subject attributes to itself, this is not the whole story. Consider Kant's absolute prohibition of suicide.[38]

т: A controversial question indeed.

a: And rightly so. Such a prohibition falls within the duties toward oneself. But when an individual considers her life so dreadful as to opt for suicide, how might one claim that this choice is precluded just by her duties toward herself? This claim can be made only because, for Kant, rationality confers on the being possessing it a sort of objective value of which subjectivity is, so to speak, the guardian and maidservant—we cannot, Kant states, under any condition destroy the rational being in our own persons. But if something—in this case, rationality—is to be preserved irrespective of the inclinations of the subjectivity that might be its bearer, then the very existence of such a thing turns out to be good in itself.

т: So your conclusion is that Kant's approach to intrinsic value is ambiguous?

a: Yes. In the first construal, its foundation appeals to subjectivity—something that, by the way, makes the idea of intrinsic value redundant, as the subject is the quintessential source of normativity. In the second construal, in contrast, the foundation of intrinsic value, being severed from subjectivity, cannot but be associated with the property of making the universe a better place just by existing—

т: And this means that, all considered, it turns out that not even in Kant can one find a "Kantian" notion of intrinsic value!

a: I daresay, Theo. For if, as a consequence of its redundancy, we exclude the first construal, what we are left with is simply the "Moorean" version.

т: You seem worried by this.

a: I am, Theo. For a theory of Moorean intrinsic value cannot but appeal to specific perspectives that may ground it—that is, that may offer a basis for the idiosyncratic idea that some particular things make the world a better place just by existing. And, as we now know well, when what is at issue is the treatment of individuals, it is unacceptable to draw universal values from arbitrary interpretations of reality. This is just what happens whenever intrinsic value is mentioned in the context of moral status.

T: You mean, when it is appealed to in order to selectively grant some individuals protection from being used merely as a means?

A: Exactly. For, once again, why should the lives of some individuals be accorded lesser value than the lives of other individuals on the ground of particular views about what is good for the universe? How can the derogatory category of "the animal" be created on the basis of idiosyncratic claims about the "intrinsic value" of rationality or self-consciousness or other? How can unverifiable metaphysical theses be appealed to in the name of treating some humans as naturally less deserving than others?[39]

T: But, Alexandra, as far as I can tell, the traditional, discredited perfectionist tendencies concerning humans do not appear in contemporary moral and political philosophy.

A: Because usually they are somehow disguised or concealed, while their open defense is confined to the sphere of human/nonhuman dealings. There is, however, a field in which forms of perfectionism embodying appeals to intrinsic value have recently openly reemerged with reference to humans as well.

T: Do you refer to bioethics?

A: Yes. But before opening this new thread of discourse, what about some sweet grapes? Or do you prefer a glass of wine?

T: Yes, please, Alexandra, some wine. Is it Greek?

A: Yes, and the color of the sea. . . .

T: Now you are teasing me.

Alexandra leaves, and comes back with the wine and some nuts. They start sipping the wine.

A: Well, then, bioethics. It is a fact that discussions about euthanasia, abortion, and infanticide have brought to the forefront the question of a possible comparative assessment of the value of different human lives. And, as you know, in this context some authors have argued for a hierarchization that puts some human individuals beyond the pale of full moral protection.

т: That certainly accounts for the fierceness of the debate. But how could they, in our egalitarian age?

A: They have taken different routes. Some, for example, in a rather traditional vein, have defended allegedly qualitative, objective viewpoints. The core idea here is that the lives of individuals may have different qualitative value according to the presence or absence of some particular cognitive skills.[40] On these views, such skills make the lives of their carriers more valuable objectively, irrespective of the prudential value they may contain—that is, irrespective of how well or badly they are going from their subjective point of view. This specification is fundamental, because bioethics deals with questions like selective infanticide for miserably disabled children and euthanasia and assisted suicide for irrevocably suffering adults, and it is clear that the assessment of the value of life in these specific cases is different from a general assessment with reference to moral status.

т: Can you explain this better?

A: The question is that, while an individual's life can rightfully be seen as liable to be taken when it is not worth living from the prudential perspective of its subject because of how much suffering it involves, this does not alter the fact that such a life is in general terms granted full moral status. That is, to say that euthanasia—voluntary or nonvoluntary—is in some cases acceptable does not mean that the life of the involved individual counts for less than the life of any other individual.

т: This seems to me to be obvious.

A: To me too . . . but unluckily it sometimes happens that, when authors working in bioethics discuss the wrongness of taking life, such a distinction gets blurred. In other words, there can be a shift from "value of life" in the sense of "value of the existence" for the individual whose life it is to "value of life" in the sense of "value of the individual" whose life it is.

т: How can this be?

A: Well, in my opinion this can happen only because the plausibility of the idea that the prudential value of an existence can vary depending on whether it is subjectively happy or miserable is surreptitiously transferred to the idea that the value of an individual's life can vary depending on the presence, or level of presence, of some favorite skills. Thus, the result is not the settling of specific bioethical dilemmas but a perfectionist approach to global problems of moral status. It seems, then, that we are back to our usual question: how are the judgments on the alleged objective variations in value among the lives of different individuals determined? The answer can only be: on the basis of the idea that the existence of individuals of such kind is somehow good for the universe—the fact that there are individuals endowed with these skills must be seen, in an absolute sense, as preferable to the fact that there are no such beings.

T: And this points to just that notion of intrinsic value that you claim is unacceptable in the context of discussion of moral status.

A: Yes, Theo, and it is discomforting to realize this. However, as I told you, this is only one of the routes that have been taken. There have been at least two other relevant perfectionistic attempts at a hierarchization of the value of life. According to the first one, only beings possessing the wish to go on living can be harmed by being killed. The harm that death is would, in this light, merely lie in the frustration of the desire for continued life.[41]

T: Whatever its other merits, here is finally an analytic approach. . . . In this case, you can't speak of ancestral legacies, can you?

A: I appreciate the way you have assimilated my line of reasoning, Theo! In fact, it is its other merits I mainly challenge. There is a but, though. . . .

T: That is?

A: Can you infer what is the cognitive skill required to harbor the desire for continued life?

T: I'd say . . . a sense of time? An awareness of oneself?

A: Why not, more simply, self-consciousness? Doesn't this have a familiar ring? It seems that, after some gyrations, we have returned to the same old point. . . . But of course this is a, so to speak, subsidiary observation. The main point is—

T: Wait, Alexandra—are we saying self-consciousness? What, then, about small children? Could they be lightheartedly killed?

A: All things being equal, yes. In the language of rights, they'd lack the right to life. And with them, nonparadigmatic humans and—but this is of course quite unsurprising—a number of nonhumans.

T: But we usually think that it's just the lives of children that must be particularly protected.

A: Indeed, Theo. And why do we do so? For a sound reason, I maintain—because we think that the loss of something may be harmful to individuals even though they are ignorant of this fact and consequently do not care about it. The main charge against the approach we are discussing is that it is based on a too restricted notion of harm. What about the idea that, since we don't have the conscious desire to breathe oxygen, we would not be harmed were we deprived of oxygen?

T: This is more than implausible.

A: But isn't this exactly like saying that, since someone doesn't have the conscious desire to go on living, she would not be harmed were she killed? Isn't this just as implausible? The value of life is for us instrumental—the continuation of our existence is important not because it is preferred or valued in itself, but because it enables us to have all that is valuable to us—experiences, emotions, activities, relationships. And the same holds, of course, for small children, for the nonparadigmatic members of our species, and for the members of other species.

T: No need to say that on this I agree. . . . On the other hand, you mentioned a further approach.

A: But aren't you tired, Theo?

T: Oh no, Alexandra—this nice breeze refreshes my brain.

A: Yes, and today it is particularly pleasant. . . . Well, the second proposal. Some authors have tried a subjective defense of perfectionism. They have argued that the lives of different individuals can be classified on the basis of the amount of their possible prudential content, that is, of the possibility for happiness or satisfaction that they imply. Thus, it has been claimed that killing an individual who has a more complex life is more objectionable than killing an individual who has a simpler life, or that the death of mentally more complex individuals, who would be deprived of a greater range of opportunities for satisfaction, is a greater harm than the death of simpler individuals. To put it in terms of the usually favored characteristics, the more autonomous, rational, communicative the individual, the richer the possible prudential value of her life.[42]

т: Might one say that behind such accounts lies something like a mathematical calculation? In other words: the greater the complexity of the individual, the greater the number of interests; the greater the number of interests, the greater the quantity of possible satisfaction; the greater the quantity of possible satisfaction, the greater the harm that the loss of life is.

а: A good synthesis, Theo.

т: It is curious—it seems that we are here facing in a straightforward way the kind of calculation in ethics that is so resolutely censured by some continental philosophers.

а: Are you thinking in particular of Jacques Derrida?

т: Yes, though not only. . . .

а: Well, in general I quite disagree with the suspicious aversion to whatever has a scientific ring to it that underlies the rejection of any application of a calculable process to ethics, oddly seen as a realm marked by "the ordeal of the undecidable."[43] In this case, however, I do think that there may be a point in the criticism. On the face of it, the appeal to quantitative aspects is less archaic than the appeal to qualitative elements. . . .

т: I'd even say that, in a sense, the history of our culture shows a tendency to abandon quality for quantity—just think of the replacement of metaphysical essentialism with evolutionary gradualism.

а: Quite so. And of course, an approach rooted in subjectivity represents an improvement with respect to allegedly objective perspectives. Yet something has gone wrong somewhere. For, within a subjective approach, the quantitative calculation cannot be made from outside. If the value one wants to measure is experiential, its greater or lesser quantity can be measured from no viewpoint other than that of the individual whose life is in question. There is no "global" subject, the experiential value of whose life is made up of the net balance of the satisfaction and the frustration of all existing individuals, and from whose perspective it would make sense to evaluate harms by comparing the more of an individual with the less of another individual.[44]

T: That's correct—but can't there be at least a neutral viewpoint from which an intraindividual comparison between lives could be reasonably made?

A: Actually, this has been suggested. But it doesn't work either. It's impossible to conceive of a truly neutral superindividual viewpoint. In order to make choices, one needs to be already endowed with preferences. And, rather than being neutral, such preferences are obviously those of the more cognitively endowed individual attempting the comparison—[45]

T: —that is, of the human—or, better yet, of the philosopher. I grasp your point! How, then, can these specific forms of perfectionism be advanced?

A: You won't be surprised by my answer, Theo. What is here at work, I hold, is a covert reference to objective, not subjective, grounds—it is, albeit implicitly, the idea that the presence of quantitatively richer lives is better from the point of view of the universe. Thus, at the end of the day, what we find is, once again, the notion of intrinsic value. Otherwise, what could prevent the appreciation of the obvious fact that if one really adopts an internal outlook for every existence in question, the evaluation of the magnitude of the harm that death is radically changes? All the more so: in this case, no comparative evaluation can be done—for each involved individual, the opportunities for satisfaction that her specific existence allows are all she has. . . . Since death means the end of everything, dying is something categorical, which cannot involve greater or lesser levels of harm.

T: All in all, it seems that intrinsic value is hard to kill even in rational ethics.

A: Yes—it is odd to realize how the archaic halo of the idea that there should be things whose mere existence is good, or better, in itself might keep bewitching our thinking. . . . It could even be amusing, if it weren't for the role that the notion still plays in discounting the lives of so many human and nonhuman beings.

Alexandra remains silent for a while. Then she starts talking again.

A: Well, Theo, I think I have now touched on all my main targets. But I'd like to put together all the objections I have advanced against perfectionism in a more organized way. . . . What about a final encounter tomorrow?

T: Oh, Alexandra, it is a wonderful idea.... In the morning?

A: Perfect. Now let's relax and finish our wine.

Epilogue

Alexandra and Theo are sitting in their chairs on the terrace. They look silently at a golden-blue lizard on the parapet. After a while, the lizard starts and quickly scurries away into a small hole between two stones. Alexandra turns to Theo. Of Tiergarten*s and* T4 *programs.*

A: She has fled.... Well, a short visit from a nonhuman just before the end of our dialogue. A despised animal, that beautiful little reptile.

T: Why do you say so?

A: You should remember.

T: Ah, of course, you are thinking of Heidegger's lizard.... The lizard sunning herself on a rock has no access to the "rock as rock"—where the "as" is the hallmark of access to beings as such.[46]

A: Perfect, as always.... Heidegger chooses just the lizard to illustrate what he deems to be the difference between human and animal being. But reptiles on rocks are favored examples not only for philosophers. I recall a prominent ethologist referring to a group of iguanas on a reef of rocks as a perfect instance of mutual indifference and total absence of friendly behavior.[47]

T: As if they had no access to the other iguanas as iguanas.

A: A nice witty remark, Theo, which points out well our obsession with finding grounds for discounting nonhumans! And, to return to our main argument, perfectionism plays a basic role in this overall process of rationalization.

T: So are you ready to offer a brief summary of your challenge?

A: Well, yes. What I have defended is the idea that perfectionism—the hierarchical arrangement of the moral status of individuals based on (the level of) possession of certain cognitive skills—is an atavism that a sound ethics can no longer accept. My argument has been largely negative. I have examined how it may be claimed that there are hierarchies in moral status based on mental skills, and have endeavored to show that none of the claims involved stands up to scrutiny. To metaphysically based ethical approaches, I have objected that great descriptive myths become dangerous when, through their embodiment of normative views, they affect fundamental questions of moral status—

T: —unduly encroaching upon the territory of social morality.

A: Perfect, Theo. Against virtue ethics, I have urged on the one hand that, having been born in connection with an aristocratic outlook, it cannot handle serious disagreements among equals, and on the other hand that deep in its structure lies a focus on moral agents that is at best unwarranted, as it blurs the distinction between the possibility of morality and the object of morality, and at worst sinister, as it sanctions, via the ideas of reciprocity and contract, lesser protection for the weak.

T: And, finally, you have attacked intrinsic value.

A: Yes. To ethical perspectives giving center stage to intrinsic value I have objected that the archaic spell of such a notion—whose many avatars allow for its covert employment even where one wouldn't imagine finding it—prevents us from clearly seeing that it has no place in discussions of moral status. For either its rootedness in subjectivity makes it redundant, or its separation from subjectivity makes it dependent on the already criticized arbitrary interpretations of the universe.

T: All this seems clear and sensible, Alexandra—but in fact what you are attacking is one of the foundation stones of mainstream Western moral philosophy.

A: And a powerful stone indeed, since, as I have suggested, the intertwining of all these ethical attitudes grants reciprocal, surreptitious plausibility to each of them, thus producing a nearly impregnable stronghold.

T: A difficult battle.

A: Yes, but consider what is at stake, Theo. I won't mention the billions of nonhumans whose sacrifice is licensed through appeals to perfectionism—this is my starting point. But, as far as humans are concerned, I have a favorite example. During the Nazi regime, and before the massive organized ethnic genocide took place in the death camps, a program called Aktion T4 was enacted in Germany. The program—code named after the address of a villa at Tiergartenstrasse 4 in Charlottenberg, where the administrative offices were placed—was initiated in 1939, and, although officially interrupted in 1941, continued covertly until 1945.[48]

T: I think I heard about it.

A: And do you remember of what it consisted?

T: It was a euthanasia program, if I remember correctly.

A: That's what the Nazis called it. In fact, it was not a euthanasia project, as it did not imply the individual administration of an easy death in the interest of the patients, but was instead a form of discriminatory mass killing—do you remember the distinction between the value of one's existence and the value of one's life? Anyhow, starting with the murder of disabled children, where "experts" made the decision whether a child was to live or die by placing a plus or minus sign on a form, the operations soon expanded to include adults— something which prompted the development of the gas chambers. It is estimated that, at the end of the war, at least 6,000 children had been killed and 180,000 adults had been eliminated in the context of Aktion T4. What, then, was the criterion for being enlisted in the program? Though some of the involved individuals had physical disabilities, the focus of Aktion T4 was on the "incurable feebleminded"— that is, on the individuals lacking the cognitive skills that, as we have seen, our philosophical tradition considers as a requirement for full moral status.

T: Do you mean that, in a sense, Aktion T4 is a consistent outcome of all our cultural history—the straightforward implementation of perfectionist attitudes?

A: Exactly. The lives of those who were killed were unworthy of living, it was claimed, because while their existence weighed heavily on the community, they were nothing but idiots, or "empty human shells." And qualification for the relevant programs—first of sterilization, then of "mercy killing"—was often determined by administering intelligence tests during which the examiners also judged the test-taker's conduct, such as eye contact, pronunciation, and rapidity of response. In other words, your IQ decided the value of your life.

T: What you are saying is rather shocking, Alexandra. And one might object that the horror we now feel in the face of such practices shows, at the very least, that the attitude behind them cannot be considered as the only, or even the main, outcome of our cultural history.

A: It is true that we now condemn Aktion T4. But we do it mainly for the wrong reason—we haven't yet learned its lesson.

T: That is?

A: If you think it over, Theo, our main objection to Aktion T4 is not straightforwardly directed against perfectionism. What do we say when we condemn it? Do we claim that it is wrong to degrade individuals on the basis of their cognitive skills? No, what we usually say is that it is wrong to degrade human beings because they are human.

T: And isn't this a sound reply?

A: It is a curious reply. For we attack one of the forms that discrimination took in Nazi ideology—the one based on cognitive level—by appealing to another of those forms—discrimination based on biological characteristics.

T: Wait, Alexandra—your argument is hard to follow, and also hard to swallow. I need some more intermediary steps.

A: Oh, in fact the argument is easier than it seems. Don't we condemn the Nazi policy of discriminating against—indeed, exploiting and killing—individuals on the basis of the biological group they belonged to? And don't we do this because we hold that scientific classifications in themselves have no bearing in ethics, and that biological characteristics such as gender or race membership have no moral relevance? And yet, when we say that humans should be morally protected *qua humans*, aren't we giving moral weight to a biological characteristic—that is, species membership?

T: Now I am beginning to follow you. And perhaps I am starting to see the next step.

A: I'm sure you see it, Theo. The next step comes by itself. We cannot reject sexism and racism while defending "speciesism."[49] We cannot put nonhumans in an inferior moral category qua nonhumans. Differently from what happens with perfectionism, one cannot, in the case of speciesism, count on a whole host of confusedly overlapping conventional views. Here, the criticism immediately cuts deep: the mere appeal to species membership simply cannot work in a context characterized by the rejection of forms of biologism. And, keeping this in mind, I can now turn to the *pars construens* of our discourse, giving you an idea of the, I'd say, "perfected" ethics that, as if reversed in a mirror, emerges as the opposite of the views I have criticized. But before this, do you need a little pause?

T: You read my mind, Alexandra. . . . And I'll use it to make a collateral comment.

A: Okay, I'm eager to hear it. But first have some of the sweet grapes you refused yesterday.

Alexandra extracts from a cup on the table two dripping clusters of grapes, and hands Theo one of them. Theo gets up, takes a few steps, and then sits on the parapet in front of her.

T: Well, I was reflecting on a age-old notion in moral philosophy—the notion of "good." But this needs a little introduction. . . . Previously, you made reference to the distinction between narrow morality and broad morality. Doesn't this correspond by and large to the traditional division of ethics into theory of conduct and theory of value? I refer, of course, to what you called overall theory of value, not to a theory of moral status.

A: In a sense, yes. . . . That's interesting.

T: And while a theory of conduct is somehow dominated by the notion of right, an overall theory of value is somehow dominated by the notion of good. . . . It is of the overall theory of value that philosophers tend to think when they define ethics as a branch of axiology. . . . It is to ethics as a branch of axiology that the notion of good is central. And I recall a description of axiology running more or less like this: axiology makes reference to an ideal hierarchy, metaphysically grounded, to which the order of human values must tend, with the aim of complying with it as far as possible.

A: I follow you—go on.

T: Couldn't we say, along the lines of our discussion so far, that the notion of good is more ancestral than the notion of right? That it is more easily connected with metaphysics, and also with the idea of intrinsic value? All things considered, we can hypostatize the Summum Bonum, or Highest Good—but we cannot make the Right into a distinct substance.

A: Very enlightening, Theo. Not coincidentally, the Summum Bonum has even been held to coincide with God. Metaphysics and religion once again hand in hand. . . . And, once again, there would be nothing to object to if these approaches kept themselves within the limits of broad morality and did not interfere with narrow morality and with questions of moral status.

T: Something very difficult to obtain, Alexandra. The great religious and metaphysical systems are essentially totalizing views.

A: Actually, that's one of the main problems a sound ethics must confront.

T: Can we now turn to the description of such sound ethics?

Theo sits again in the chair next to Alexandra. He must shield his eyes for a while, to reaccustom them to the brightness of the sea.

A: With pleasure, Theo. But first, a little background. Reaching the point where we presently stand has required a turn in our thinking. Today, as your reaction to Aktion T4 shows, it is normal for us to think that our life has no lesser value than the life of a Nobel prize winner, or that the life of a child with Down syndrome has no lesser value than our life. Yet it is clear that this hasn't seemed natural for centuries.

T: And what made the turn possible?

A: In my opinion, there have been two major changes. The first one, going back at least to Henry Sidgwick, is the idea of the autonomy of ethics—the view that ethics is a theoretical inquiry endowed with its own standards of justification, within which criteria coming from other domains—be they religious, metaphysical, or scientific—have no direct relevance.[50] The other, following as we know the decline of positivist skeptical influence, is the introduction into normative ethics of that analytic method marked by clarity and explicit argumentation that had already substantiated attacks on metaphysics in other branches of philosophy. It is to these elements, I think, that we owe all the main substantive achievements I've amply used in our discussion.

T: For example?

A: For example, the idea that, when what is at stake is basic moral treatment, there is no room for the arbitrariness of general belief systems. Or the realization that the class of beings who can deserve moral protection does not logically coincide with the class of beings who can act morally. And, of course, the claim that, through their having positive and negative attitudes toward what happens to them, subjects are the only immediate and uncontroversial sources of value, characterized by an equal, basic negative prescription: do not harm me. Now, the perspective I want to point to is somehow molded by these views. And, curiously enough, it is not an eccentric theory, but rather the most universally accepted among contemporary ethical doctrines—human rights theory.

T: That's intriguing.

A: First, human rights doctrine avoids the confusion between broad and narrow morality, and essentially focuses on the special class of moral concerns having to do with the basic, institutional protection of individuals from interference—hence, its stress on the fundamental negative rights to life, freedom, and welfare. Second, the criterion for access to the sphere of rights holders is simply the fact of being an agent, that is, an intentional being that has goals and wants to achieve them.

T: Does this mean that neither rationality nor self-consciousness nor conceptual-linguistic abilities are required?

A: Exactly. As a result, human rights doctrine clears the way both of any form of perfectionism connected with specific hierarchical worldviews and of any selective focus on moral agents.

T: In other words, it gets rid both of great myths and of the master/slave dichotomy. What about intrinsic value?

A: Admittedly, it sometimes happens—especially, but not only, in political manifestoes—that reminiscences of the Kantian concept of dignity somehow reintroduce conventional references to intrinsic value. But in its best philosophical foundation, human rights theory, far from embodying the traditional, metaphysically oriented notion of intrinsic value, achieves both the reweaving of the connection between intrinsic value and subjectivity and the development of a radically egalitarian framework. On the one hand, it sees intrinsic value only in something as subjective as the satisfaction of the fundamental interests—in freedom, in welfare, and in life as a precondition for them—of intentional beings. And on the other hand, it grants equal intrinsic value to the satisfaction of these interests, as it recognizes that they are equally vital from the subjective perspective of their holders.

T: From this, the attribution of equal rights, irrespective of sex, race—

A: —and cognitive endowment. The end of intrahuman perfectionism.

T: But not, it seems, of perfectionism without qualifications. In the case of animals—

A: Exactly so, Theo. Deeply ingrained moral doctrines—especially when they are complacently self-serving—do not lose their hold from one day to the next. Why have we come to define the particular sort of equal moral claims that I have just described as "human rights"? Why have we excluded all nonhuman individuals from their protection, thus allowing for their unimpeded confinement and killing?

T: Well, I suppose the answer cannot be because they aren't human. That would be, I agree, blatant speciesism. And speciesism not only is, as you suggested, inconsistent with our moral framework but also, since we are speaking of archaisms, would bring us back to one of the most ancestral of our moral ideas—the sinister notion of the sacral significance of "blood and race." . . . No ethics deserving the name can accept this.

A: Unquestionable. Thus, it is not difficult to identify where the burden of proof for the exclusion of nonhumans lies—with perfectionism. In the very field where, in the intrahuman case, its uncertain steps are hotly debated and deeply resisted—bioethics—perfectionism is overtly stressed when it comes to nonhuman beings. And on a more general level, while exacting mental skills don't any longer play a role in our current morality, so that mere intentionality is the criterion for having human rights, most philosophers are ready—indeed, eager—to defend the old perfectionist criteria and to put them to use when dealing with nonhumans.

T: I was thinking of a curious thing, Alexandra. Casually, Aktion T4 borrowed its name from a street named after the presence of an animal-exploiting institution—*Tiergarten* means "zoo." It's almost as if there were a link trying to get to the surface.

A: An acute observation, Theo. And a link there is. It is, of course, perfectionism. The primeval category of "the animal" is at the same time the first and the last stronghold of perfectionism. Only the death of "the animal" will allow for the liberation of animals.

T: Are you envisaging a society where no nonhuman individual is legally confined or killed?

A: I am envisaging it, Theo—but it's our ethical reasoning that has paved the way for it. Peter Singer has a striking image for this phenomenon. He has observed that beginning to reason is like stepping onto an escalator that leads upward and out of sight—once we take the first step, the distance to be traveled is independent of our will.[51]

T: Oh, Alexandra, on your part you have led me far indeed!

A: I am aware of this. And I thank you for the good company you bore me along the way.

T: But I'm sure this won't be enough for you, because you rightly think that ethics is a practical discipline, whose conclusions are not only theories but also actions. . . .

Alexandra smiles silently, looking at the sea. Then she turns again to Theo.

A: I know that you are leaving tomorrow, Theo. Shall we have a last swim?

Roundtable

I

Humanist and Posthumanist Antispeciesism

CARY WOLFE

I'M NOT A philosopher, much less an analytic philosopher, so I've never had much use—even less, perhaps, than Paola Cavalieri herself—for the idea of "moral perfectionism." For a nonphilosopher who isn't invested in the technical nuances thereof, the term itself is bound to sound, well, a little self-flattering—a fantasy, even, that the "human" has of itself (a point I'll return to in a moment). To paraphrase Kenneth Burke in the 1930s, philosophers who take such a term seriously are bound to find sooner or later (and we hope it is sooner) that their ideas are too good for this world, and hence Burke called for "a shift of emphasis from 'good times' to 'bad times' as the norm," for the simple reason that "virtues are by very definition rare and exceptional."[1] So rather than worrying about "perfecting" anything, maybe we would do better to start with more modest goals, like not destroying the planet, or not brutalizing nonhuman animals by the millions each year. Such, I take it, is the impulse of Cavalieri's admirably circumspect attitude toward moral perfectionism.

The fact that I'm not an analytical philosopher also allows me to couch my remarks here somewhat at a tangent to much of Cavalieri's wonderfully clear and concise dialogue, which manages to walk us through many of the main arguments and positions in analytic philosophy regarding our ethical duties to (at least some) nonhuman animals. That this proviso—"at least some"—is not taken up here is no doubt a matter of the sheer demands of economy of the format, but it is, I think, an important question that yields considerable dividends when we do pay attention to it.

The first thing it does is move us away from thinking about nonhuman animals in a generic, one-size-fits-all fashion, which itself only reinforces the human/animal dichotomy that, as Cavalieri rightly notes, is hard-wired to the idea of moral perfectionism. As a very different kind of philosopher, Jacques Derrida, exclaimed in a late essay, the *"animal, what a word!,"* because buried under the definite article here is all the heterogeneity that makes the starfish so different from the ring-tailed lemur, the eel from the zebra (and that makes *Homo sapiens*, by the way, closer kin to the bonobo and the chimpanzee than those great apes are to many of their fellow "animals"). In fact, Derrida writes, "each time a philosopher, or anyone else says, 'the Animal' in the singular and without further ado, claiming thus to designate every thing that is held not to be man," he (and given the logic he is criticizing here, it must be "he") "utters an *asininity*," and so confirms "not only the animality that he is disavowing but his complicit, continued and organized involvement in a veritable war of the species"—a war that Derrida compares in that same essay (as J. M. Coetzee and his character Elizabeth Costello do) to the genocide of World War II, one whose *"unprecedented* proportions" are most obvious, perhaps, in factory farming.[2]

This question—the specific attributes and qualities of different kinds of animals, human and nonhuman—is also an important methodological one that has bearing upon Cavalieri's attempt on the one hand to criticize metaphysics and "onto-theology" (to use Richard Rorty's characterization of Heidegger's work) and, on the other, to enlist scientific knowledges in the service of her argument without at the same time falling into "biological continuism" (to use Derrida's phrase) and indulging one of the cardinal sins of ethics that goes under the name, as she reminds us here, of "Hume's Law": deriving ethical principles and concepts from empirical and scientific observations.

Within the terms of her own argument, this is one of the junctures where I might register a quibble or two, for it isn't at all clear to me that Cavalieri's position doesn't indeed derive ethical directives from empirical observations (in this case, observations of a particular animal's behavioral repertoire, capacities, and so on)—a problem that the phrase "direct" derivation is intended perhaps to paper over (see pp. 6, 8).[3] Similarly, one might object to the strategic partition between "morality in the broad sense" and "morality in the narrow sense" (pp. 9–10) and ask if "precepts about the good life, the character traits to be fostered, the values to be pursued" and so on can ever (or *should* ever) be separated from "a system of constraints on conduct . . . whose task is to protect the interests of others." I'll return to this point in a moment, but *both* of these moralities, broad and narrow, I would say, "leave room for the arbitrariness of specific worldviews"—a fact that doesn't exclude stringent requirements for justification, but just changes what justification might look like.

But I'm not especially interested here in offering counterpoints or challenges to Cavalieri's argument within the terrain of analytic philosophy itself, for on balance, it seems to me that if you agree with her about what philosophy is, and if you agree with her about what ethics is, then her work (here and in her book *The Animal Question*) has gone about as far as you can go in convincingly making the case for the ethical standing of animals and in laying out the philosophical foundations for granting (at least some of) them rights within the existing juridical and political frameworks. Indeed, the most winning aspect of her work, to me, is its circumscription and its pragmatism, its ability to take the existing philosophical and legal edifice of liberalism at its own word and show, very patiently and very clearly, how it *requires*, if it is to be internally consistent, our recognition of the standing of (at least some) nonhuman animals.

But it seems odd, to me at least, that a philosophical orientation such as hers would be presented in the form of a *dialogue*—that oldest of philosophical (or is it literary?) forms that would seem to unsettle the boundary between philosophy and literature in ways whose implications are not to be underestimated. For it is a critical commonplace, I suppose, to ask whether and how, in the dialogue form, we can know how much of the project's success is due to the logical and propositional force of the argument (which is not reducible to the second-order, cosmetic operations of language, or so the story would go), and how much to the linguistic and literary means of persuasion (including those strange pauses and interludes, in the dialogue and yet not in it, where one fetches some grapes or goes for a swim, and god knows what else transpires between the interlocutors). To put it as baldly as possible, if reason is and does what the dialogue says, then why couch it in the form of a dialogue *at all*? So the dialogue form would seem to exemplify particularly well what Derrida famously calls "the logic of the supplement"—the need to complete a thing (why else use it?) that is, supposedly, already self-sufficient and self-contained, as argument, in its propositional force.

The intricated, interfolded relationship between philosophy and literature has been explored with particular subtlety by a number of philosophers, of course, including Stanley Cavell, who notes that "literary" has often, within professional philosophical circles, been used as a code word for "nonserious" and "nonphilosophical" (nowhere more frustratingly, for Cavell, than in the reception of the figure most important to him, Ralph Waldo Emerson). I mention Cavell here in part because his version of moral perfectionism is rather askance to the usual sense of the term that Cavalieri explains to us here. Cavell recognizes, on the one hand, the commonplace that "any perfectionism—democratic or aristocratic, secular or religious, philosophical or debased—will claim to have found a way of life from whose perspective all other ways of life are judged as wanting."[4] But at the same time, he is concerned to argue "that the outlook is not essentially elitist" (xxiv), because that "way of life" is not something that one can accomplish or occupy, once and for all. And it is (even more specifically) *especially* not settling on, once and for all, a set of reasons or a position from which such judgments (of "other ways of life as wanting") might be derived. He takes issue with philosopher John Rawls's "claim that a rational plan of life is one that can be lived 'above reproach.' It is this claim, above all, I think that my understanding of . . . Perfectionism contests" (xxiv). Instead, perfectionism in his view "has its foundation in rethinking" (xxix), a rethinking that is set against the Rawlsian "fantasy of a noumenal self" (the "true self," as Rawls puts it, borrowing from Kant), those selves who are assumed to have "a desire to express their nature as rational and equal members of the intelligible realm" (qtd. xxxiii).

Cavell has all sorts of problems with this position, including the fact that "the fantasy of the noumenal self as one's true self seems to me rather to be a certain expression or interpretation of the fantasy of selflessness . . . ; the idea would be that the end of all attainable selves is the absence of self, or partiality" (xxxiv). (Indeed, what could be more "partial," Cavell might add, than the norms and conventions of professional academic analytical philosophy, whose social, institutional, and historical overdeterminations are not difficult to specify?) "Such an idea," he continues, "seems rather something imposed from outside on oneself, as from another who has a use for oneself on condition that one is beyond desire, beyond change" (xxxiv). And this helps clarify what Cavell means when he speaks of "Perfectionism not as a competing moral theory (say requiring a principle of justice or ordering of principles different from the proposals of Rawls) but as emphasizing a dimension of the moral life any theory of it may wish to accommodate" (xxxi).

What Cavell's revisionist understanding of perfectionism rejects in Rawls is also, I think, what it would reject in Cavalieri's dialogue: that the partitioning of morality in the "narrow" sense from morality in the "broad" sense takes for granted (procedurally, as it were) the fantasy of a noumenal self in the sense that it assumes the self making such judgments is just a generic anybody, an idea (so the argument would go) that just further masks (but also expresses) its own forms of "partiality." So perfectionism's contribution to moral theory for Cavell is thus not about the achievement of certainty via reason deployed by such a phantasmatic noumenal self, but rather about how that fantasy covers over a key component, maybe *the* key component, of morality: the self's confrontation with itself. Typically, Cavell writes, moral theory regards "the moral creature as one that demands and recognizes the intelligibility of others to himself or herself . . . so moral conduct can be said to be based on reason; and philosophers will sometimes gloss this as the idea that moral conduct is subject to questions whose answers take the form of giving reasons" (xxxi). But moral perfectionism's contribution is about the difficulty of making oneself intelligible to *oneself* rather than asking others for reasons (or providing them) for conduct—a difficulty that the assimilation of morality to reasoning alone evades or "deflects" (to use a term from Cavell that we'll unpack more below).

Of "becoming intelligible to oneself," "making oneself intelligible (one's actions, one's sufferings, one's position)" Cavell writes, it is "as if the threat to one's moral coherence comes most insistently from that quarter, from one's sense of obscurity to oneself, as if we are subject to demands we cannot formulate, leaving us unjustified, as if our lives condemn themselves" (xxxii). And perfectionism's contribution is to confront us with "this search for intelligibility, or say this search for direction in what seems a scene of moral chaos, the scene of the dark place in which one has lost one's way" (xxxii). But this doesn't mean that we are thereby relieved of ethical responsibility; on the contrary, it means that it must be navigated, negotiated, and lived up to every day, because one's ethical "position" is not a place that one arrives at and settles into once and for all; it is not, with Heidegger, a form of "dwelling," but rather, with Emerson, a form of "abandonment" or "onwardness." Not a destination but, as Cavell says, a "task."

Cavell's characterization of perfectionism is bodied forth, if we believe philosopher Cora Diamond, in J. M. Coetzee's Elizabeth Costello (and also, I would suggest, in his character David Lurie in *Disgrace*), which accounts, Diamond argues, for Costello's rawness and "woundedness." In an important scene, she is asked by the president of the university whether her vegetarianism "comes out of moral conviction," and she responds, against the expectations of her hosts, "no, I don't think so. . . . It comes out of a desire to save my soul." And when the university administrator politely replies, "Well, I have a great respect for it," she retorts, "I'm wearing leather shoes. I'm carrying a leather purse. I wouldn't have overmuch respect if I were you."[5] From Diamond's point of view, what haunts Costello here is not just the weight and scale of our brutality toward animals in practices such as factory farming, but also a *second* kind of trauma: the limits of our own reason in confronting such a reality, being able to process it—the trauma, as Diamond puts it, of "experiences in which we take something in reality to be resistant to our thinking it, or possibly to be painful in its inexplicability."[6] In Diamond's terms, to mistake "the difficulty of philosophy" (a propositional and as it were technical difficulty) for this "difficulty of reality" (as Diamond suggests is the case with the philosophical "Reflections" published at the end of Coetzee's *The Lives of Animals*) is to indulge in a "deflection" of a reality that impinges upon us in ways not masterable by reason and the crafting of analytical arguments. (That is why, she suggests, Elizabeth Costello doesn't offer one in defense of her vegetarianism; and it is also why Coetzee's character is very quick to point to the inconsistency of her own practices with regard to animal products.) Moreover, Diamond suggests, Coetzee brilliantly uses the *difference* between literature and philosophy in *The Lives of Animals* to dramatize just this point in ways mostly missed by the philosophical commentaries that follow it.

For Diamond, then, the duty of moral thinking is above all *not* to deflect what Cavell calls our "exposure" to the world—a deflection that, she suggests, might well be rooted in our own sense of *physical* exposure to vulnerability and mortality that links us to our fellow creatures and forms the basis of our moral response to them. As Diamond puts it in a key moment in her essay, unpacking her sense of Costello's startling assertion that "I know what it is like to be a corpse":

> The awareness we each have of being a living body, being "alive to the world," carries with it exposure to the bodily sense of vulnerability to death, sheer animal vulnerability, the vulnerability we share with them. This vulnerability is capable of panicking us. To be able to acknowledge it at all, let alone as shared, is wounding; but acknowledging it as shared with other animals, in the presence of what we do to them, is capable not only of panicking one but also of isolating one, as Elizabeth Costello is isolated. Is there any difficulty in seeing why we should not prefer to return to moral debate, in which the livingness and death of animals enter as facts that we treat as relevant in this or that way, not as presences that may unseat our reason? ("Difficulty" 74)

This is part of the reason that Diamond rejects rights philosophy (pro or con) in thinking about our moral obligations to animals. For her, the fundamental question of *justice* issues from an essentially different conceptual realm than the question of "rights." "When genuine issues of justice and injustice are framed in terms of rights," she argues, "they are thereby distorted and trivialized" because of "the underlying tie between rights and a system of entitlement that is concerned, not with evil done to a person, but with how much he or she gets compared to other participants in the system."[7] In rights discourse, she argues, "the *character* of our conflicts is made obscure" by what Wittgenstein would call a poor grammatical description of the problem we are trying to confront ("Injustice" 124).

What the rights tradition misses, in her view, then, is that the "capacity to respond to injustice as injustice" depends not on working out (from a safe ontological distance, as it were, the space of Rawls's noumenal self) who should have a fair share of this or that abstract "good," based upon the possession of this or that abstract "interest" or attribute, but rather on "a recognition of *our own* vulnerability"—a recognition not demanded and in some sense actively avoided by rights-oriented thinking ("Injustice" 121). (And here, of course, we would do well to remember the "wounded" aspect of Coetzee's Costello, a rawness that pushes her moral response to our treatment of animals beyond propositional argument—and sometimes beyond the decorum of polite society.) What such an insight points toward, Diamond contends, is the fact that "there is something wrong with the contrast, taken to be exhaustive, between demanding one's rights and begging for kindness— begging for what is *merely* kindness. The idea that *those* are the only possibilities is . . . one of the main props of the idea that doing injustice *is* failing to respect rights" (129). Contemporary moral theory thus "pushes apart justice, on the one hand, and compassion, love, pity, tenderness, on the other" (131). But Diamond's understanding of the question "has at its center the idea that a kind of loving attention to another being, a possible victim of injustice, is essential to any understanding of the evil of injustice" (131–32). In fact, she agrees with Simone Weil's suggestion that "rights can work for justice or for injustice," that the concept of rights possesses "a kind of moral noncommitment to the good" (128). In an important sense, then, "rights" are beside the point of justice per se, and "the language of rights is, one might say, meant to be useful in contexts in which we cannot count on the kind of understanding of evil that depends on loving attention to the victim" (139). (It is those contexts, I take it, that Cavalieri's circumscription of the problem is, pragmatically speaking, meant to address.)

There are, then, two different and in fact incommensurable kinds of value here ("Injustice" 121)—a point missed by *both* "sides" of what Diamond calls "that great arena of dissociated thought, contemporary debate about animals' rights."[8] The problem with both sides of the debate is that they are locked into a model of justice in which a being does or does not have rights on the basis of its possession (or lack) of morally significant characteristics that can be empirically derived. Both sides argue "that what is involved in moral thought is knowledge of empirical similarities and differences, and the testing and application of general principles of evaluation."[9] And so, as she puts it, "the opposite sides in the debate may have more in common then they realize. In the voices we hear in the debate about animal rights . . . there is a shared desire for a 'because': because animals are this kind of being, or because they are that kind of being, thus-and-such is their standing for our moral thought" ("Difficulty" 71). But what Diamond hears in both sets of voices is an evasion of our "exposure" to an arena of moral complexity in which (to quote Cavell) "The other can present me with no mark or feature on the basis of which I can *settle* my attitude" (qtd. in "Difficulty" 71).

The views of Cavell and Diamond in general—and that last quotation from Cavell in particular—are bound to remind some readers of a view of ethics that is also shared by Derrida (and, to a large extent, by poststructuralist philosophy generally): that the question of justice is not reducible to the question of rights—or to the immanence of any juridico-political doctrine. As Derrida explains in a famous passage from his essay "Force of Law," which is cited in part by Cavalieri in her dialogue:

> A decision that did not go through the ordeal of the undecidable would not be a free decision, it would only be the programmable application or unfolding of a calculable process. It might be legal; it would not be just. . . . And once the ordeal of the undecidable is past (if that is possible), the decision has again followed a rule or given itself a rule, invented it or reinvented, reaffirmed it, it is no longer *presently* just, fully just.[10]

Derrida would find in the utilitarian calculus of animal rights philosopher Peter Singer, for example, just such a "calculation," one that would actually reduce ethics to the *antithesis* of ethics by relying upon a one-size-fits-all formula for conduct that thus actually *relieves* us of ethical responsibility—an application that, in principle, could be carried out by a machine. For Derrida, then, justice is in an important sense impossible—it is a "horizon" against which law operates—but it is in this very impossibility that the possibility of justice per se resides. And it is not, I think, a "suspicious aversion to whatever has a scientific ring to it" that motivates Derrida here, as Cavalieri's dialogue suggests, but rather the fact that "the law of Law" (as Derrida calls it) always involves our confrontation with an ethical situation that is always precisely *not* generic (hence its demand and, in a sense, its trauma); it obeys instead a double articulation in which the difference between law and justice is always confronted in *specific* situations whose details matter a great deal. The "law of Law" obeys an iterability that "remains *heterogeneous*" to, rather than simply opposed to, the order of the ideal, the calculable, and so on.

Therefore, the "law of Law" names a form of ethical responsibility that entails vigilant attention to each specific, interfolded iteration of "rule and event," to "*this particular* undecidable" that "opens the field of decision or decidability," one that "is always a *determinate* oscillation between possibilities." The moment of ethics thus takes place "in strictly *defined* situations (for example, discursive—syntactical or rhetorical—but also political, ethical, etc.)" that "are *pragmatically* determined."[11] And they involve "an act of justice that must always concern singularity, individuals, irreplaceable groups and lives . . . in a unique situation" ("Force of Law" 17). Were I content just to apply a generic rule, "I would act, Kant would say, *in conformity* with duty, but not *through* duty or *out of respect* for the law" ("Force of Law" 17).

This is not to say that Derrida doesn't care about the questions usually associated with the term "animal rights." He clearly does, and nowhere more forcefully than in his later work. In an interview from 2004, for instance, he insists that "this industrial, scientific, technical violence will not be tolerated for very much longer, neither de facto nor de jure. . . . The relations between humans and animals *must* change. They *must* both in the sense of an 'ontological' necessity and of an 'ethical' duty. I place these words in quotation marks because this change will have to affect the very sense and value of these concepts (the ontological and the ethical)."[12] This helps to clarify in turn why Derrida thinks that the existing framework of rights cannot accommodate these concerns—why it even, in some sense, actively mitigates against them. "For the moment," he suggests, "we ought to limit ourselves to working out the rules of law [*droit*] such as they exist. But it will eventually be necessary to reconsider the history of this law and to understand that although animals cannot be placed under concepts like citizen, consciousness linked with speech . . . etc., they are not for all that without a 'right.' It's the very concept of right that will have to be 'rethought'" ("Violence Against Animals" 73–74).

Derrida's point here is not just the obvious one that we "cannot expect 'animals' to be able to enter into an expressly juridical contract in which they would have duties, in an exchange of recognized rights" (the Rawlsian framework that Cavalieri rightly rejects) but rather (and more pointedly) that "it is within this philosophico-juridical space that the modern violence against animals is practiced, a violence that is at once contemporary with and indissociable from the discourse of human rights." And from this vantage, it makes sense to conclude, as Derrida does, that "however much sympathy I may have for a declaration of animals' rights that would protect them from human violence," it is nevertheless "preferable not to introduce this problematic concerning the relations between humans and animals into the *existing* juridical framework" ("Violence Against Animals" 74–75). In the end, then, Derrida seems torn between the desire to work within "the rules of law such as they exist" to address the mistreatment of animals that he detests and his commitment to maintaining the full force of the "animal question" and its implications for ontology and for ethics, a force that he thinks should impel a radical and fundamental questioning of the existing juridico-political framework and its philosophical underpinnings—a project of revolutionary proportions that might, he suggests, be foreclosed by prematurely accommodating the demands of the "animal question" within the existing frameworks of politics and law.

At the center of those frameworks is, of course, a certain fantasy figure of *the human* to which we have already made reference, one that the human "gives to itself," as he puts it, in denial of its own vulnerability and finitude. Such is the full resonance, I think, of Derrida's reading of Jeremy Bentham's famous contention that the fundamental ethical question with animals is not, can they talk? or, can they reason?, but can they *suffer?*, from which he draws something quite different from Peter Singer's derivation of animals' fundamental "interests." For Derrida, putting the question this way "changes everything," because philosophy from Aristotle to Levinas has posed the question of the animal in terms of capacities (prototypically, for reason or language), which in turn "determines so many others concerning *power* or *capability* [*pou-voirs*], and *attributes* [*avoirs*]: being able, having the power to give, to die, to bury one's dead, to dress, to work, to invent a technique" ("The Animal" 386, 395). "As soon as such a question is posed," he continues, "what counts is not only the idea of a transitivity or activity (being able to speak, to reason, and so on); the important thing is rather what impels it towards self-contradiction, something we will later relate back to auto-biography" and to "*this* auto-definition, *this* auto-apprehension, *this* auto-situation of man or of the human . . . with respect to what is living and with respect to animal life" ("The Animal" 396, 393, emphasis in original).

What Derrida has in mind by the "auto-" of "auto-biography" is exemplified, as I have already suggested, in the picture of the human that is taken for granted in analytic philosophy's attempt to think our ethical relations to animals in terms of rights—a point that we have already seen Cavell making (in his response to Rawls) and Diamond elaborating (in her rejection of the philosophical commentaries appended to *The Lives of Animals*). For Derrida's crucial point (and it has immense methodological consequences for philosophy) is that there are *two* kinds of finitude here, *two* kinds of passivity and vulnerability, and that, moreover, the first type (physical vulnerability, embodiment, and, eventually, mortality) is only ever experienced by means of a second type of "passivity" or "not being able," which is the finitude we experience in our subjection to a radically ahuman technicity or mechanicity of language. This technicity has profound consequences, of course, for what we too hastily think of as "our" concepts, which are therefore in an important sense not "ours" at all.

Derrida's point, then, would be not only that "we" therefore *don't* have a concept of "the human" (noumenal or otherwise) but also that it's a good thing too, because it is only on the strength of that weakness, you might say, that we are able to avoid both horns of the dilemma that are everywhere in evidence in Cavalieri's dialogue: on the one hand, the constant threat of ethnocentrism with which a nonanalytic approach (and a certain understanding of Wittgenstein) flirts (which at the same time, however, keeps us from lapsing into "biological continuism"); and, on the other hand, the mining for ethical "universals" that, for philosophers in the rights tradition, would attempt to counter this very threat by uncovering first principles of ethics via the antiethnocentric autonomy of "reason" (but only, it seems, by courting that very continuism and flouting "Hume's Law").

Derrida, I am suggesting, attempts to make available a "third way," whose response would be that, yes, it is true that what we think of as the "principles" of personhood, morality, and so on are inseparable from who "we" are, from our discourse as a "mode of life" (to put it in Wittgenstein's terms). But at the same time, "we" are not "we"; we are not that "auto-" of the "autobiography" that humanism "gives to itself." Rather, "we" are always radically other, already in- or ahuman in our very being—not just in the evolutionary, biological, and zoological fact of our physical embodiment, vulnerability, and mortality, of course, but also in our subjection to and constitution in the materiality and technicity of a language that is always on the scene before we are, as a precondition of our subjectivity. And this means that "what *he* calls 'man,'" what "we" call "we," always covers over a more radical "not being able" that makes our very conceptual life possible.

Even more important, perhaps—at least for the topic at hand—is that this passivity and subjection is shared by humans and nonhumans the moment they begin to interact and communicate by means of any semiotic system. As Derrida puts it in a well-known passage from the interview "Eating Well,"

> If one reinscribes language in a network of possibilities that do not merely encompass it but mark it irreducibly from the inside, everything changes. I am thinking in particular of the mark in general, of the trace, of iterability, of *différance*. These possibilities or necessities, without which there would be no language, *are themselves not only human*. . . . And what I am proposing here should allow us to take into account scientific knowledge about the complexity of "animal languages," genetic coding, all forms of marking within which so-called human language, as original as it might be, does not allow us to "cut" once and for all where we would in general like to cut.[13]

So my final point here would not be the obvious one that we are dealing in the end with two very different—in fact, absolutely opposed—ideas of what ethics is, each with its quite obvious strengths and vulnerabilities. My final and perhaps less obvious point is that the issues of (post)humanism and (anti)speciesism work themselves out on not just one but two levels: not just (to use J. L. Austin's handy terms) the constative one of what a philosophy says, in its expressed content and themes, about humans and animals, their similarities or differences and the ethical relevance thereof, and so on, but also the performative level of what a philosophy *does* (and thinks it *can* do) on a methodological level, which entails attending with particular rigor to the relationship between concepts and language. And it is here, in this second sense, that a philosophy may unwittingly reproduce a certain picture of the human that may foreclose the very project it says it wants to pursue (namely, to break down the division—or at least the taken-for-granted division—between ethical subjects based upon their species designation). From this vantage, the differences between Cavalieri's view and, say, Rawls's (which would matter immensely and indeed decisively to Cavalieri) are of little moment in comparison with their similarities.

Hence, one kind of apparently posthumanist antispeciesism—Cavalieri's kind (which is certainly posthumanist in comparison with, say, Rawls)—turns out from another point of view (namely, Derrida's) to really be a form of humanist antispeciesism. It *thinks* it is posthumanist because it seeks to find, via the autonomy and impartiality of "reason," antispeciesist principles that are taken to *be* posthumanist precisely because only such a procedure, it thinks, can rise above the ethnocentrism and socially and historically bound prejudices that make us treat animals the way we do. But from another point of view, however—not just Derrida's but also that of the more adventurous corners of the analytical tradition that accommodate Diamond and Cavell—that procedure, and that view of what philosophy and ethics are, is a quintessential form of humanism that is, ironically, part of the very problem it wants to think through.[14] It wants to be antispeciesist, but because it is already humanist, it really can't be—or rather, it can, but only in a strategic, pragmatic way. Of course, Cavalieri would say that this qualification—"strategic and pragmatic"—is precisely the point, the source of her approach's strength, its chance to make a difference. And, in a way, who could argue with that?

No Escape

HARLAN B. MILLER

LEXANDRA LEADS THEO toward the rejection of perfectionism with a number of mutually reinforcing arguments and analogies, from both philosophy and history. Theo is an intelligent man, sufficiently intelligent to see that following her to the end would require substantial changes in his life. And of course he has been around long enough to realize that not every plausible argument is in fact sound, and to hope that he can avoid her conclusion, or at least the inconvenient consequences.

I propose to demonstrate to Theo that there is no escape and that even if we grant, without argument, priority to human interests, the practical implications are indeed consequential, but not necessarily inconvenient. I will do so by recapitulating some of Alexandra's points in somewhat different ways, touching on some other considerations pro and con that may be deployed to dismiss or denigrate nonhuman interests, and showing that Alexandra's conclusions still stand. Their implications depend upon the relative weights of human and nonhuman interests and the extent of conflict between them. Those will be my last topics.

But first let us distinguish between a hierarchy and a dichotomy. A dichotomy provides for exactly two classes, mutually exclusive and within their domain jointly exhaustive. Living or dead. Citizen or noncitizen. Edible or inedible. A hierarchy, in contrast, allows for multiple ranked levels of status. General, colonel, lieutenant colonel, major, captain, etc. Male citizen, female citizen, citizen child, resident alien, slave. The first of these examples is a linear ranking, the second may or may not be, depending on the society.

Dichotomy

The distinction is of some importance here. There are some thinkers, Kantians, contractarians, perhaps a residual Cartesian or two, who divide the moral universe into dichotomous classes: fully autonomous moral agents vs. gravel and its moral equivalents, or contractors and noncontractors, or the conscious and the nonconscious. In each case, one class constitutes the totality of moral agents and patients, and members of the other class (chimpanzees, cats, dandelions, bricks) have no moral significance whatever. Most of us, however, have multistep hierarchical views, usually quite muddled, in which some things just don't matter morally and others do, but some more than others.

That nonhuman animals are conscious and capable of happiness and suffering, or at least pleasure and pain, almost no one denies. It is well established that the neurological mechanism of pain is the same in all vertebrates. At least one species of invertebrate, the octopus, behaves with a skill, sensitivity, and complexity that makes it very difficult to deny that it can be conscious. Ignoring more difficult cases, consider our fellow mammals. Set aside our close primate cousins. One can doubt the pleasure of the cat dozing in the sun, the expectation of the excited dog, the terror of the cornered mouse only if blinded by dogma. If cruelty to animals is possible, as the existence of anticruelty legislation presumes, animals must be able to suffer. Only those really in the grip of a theory can actually believe that animals (at least the other mammals) are automata.[1] Of course, extreme behaviorists of a type now almost extinct believed that there was nothing "behind" animal behavior, but they believed the same of human behavior.

To have any chance of plausibility, defenders of a human/nonhuman moral dichotomy must hold that although animal suffering (and happiness) are real, they are morally insignificant either absolutely or relative to human experience (in the latter case the distinction between hierarchy and dichotomy is trivial). There must, then, be something humans have and nonhumans lack that produces this radical difference in status. Here are a few of the candidates that have been offered: full autonomous personhood, language, self-consciousness, souls, the ability to make contracts.

The truly autonomous member of Kant's kingdom of ends acts in accordance with principles she prescribes to herself. She continually reflects, not just upon the means to her ends, but upon her ends and preferences, to see that they are in line with her meta-preferences about her preferences, which themselves must align with the laws she prescribes. Since most humans, most of the time, and some humans, all of the time, are not in such a state, this justification of the superiority of human interests is certainly vulnerable to the argument from species overlap (of which see below), but there is a more fundamental objection. No doubt the suffering or happiness or preferences or choices of such hypersophisticated agents are of value. But more than mere assertion is required to show that such states are tremendously more valuable than the unreflective happiness of the grazing manatee, or the unthinking devotion and self-sacrifice of the plover (or human) parent. Here philosophers in the analytic tradition can be found pronouncing on the sanctity of the individual person and the inviolability of persons with a dogmatism and a disdain for argument worthy of Heidegger.

Descartes famously claimed, as evidence that nonhumans were mere machines, that all humans and no nonhumans possessed genuine language.[2] In its simple form this has been disproved repeatedly, with evidence from parrots, vervet monkeys, dolphins, whales, educated chimpanzees and other apes, etc.[3] The response, invariably, has not been to abandon the claim but to redefine "real" language. In consequence, since there are humans with no or negligible language skills, this position has become more and more vulnerable to the species overlap argument.

Another move is to grant that nonhumans are conscious but deny that they are self-conscious, and then to argue that simple consciousness is morally insignificant in itself. Only reflective consciousness of consciousness, in this story, is really good or bad for the being. However, both the basic claims here are false. Simple consciousness of pain and pleasure matters. If pain were not aversive, it would not be pain and thus would serve no purpose (and there would be no mobile animals). There is a fundamental intuition here. Even though the capacity for pain is a good thing, occurrent pain is bad.

Further, it is clear that many animals are self-conscious. Bonobos and chimpanzees have shown quite complex degrees of self-awareness. But mice and young kittens never mistake their own limbs for the furniture. There are perhaps some superdeluxe forms of self-consciousness beyond the reach of any nonhuman, but these are enjoyed by a few mystics and philosophers for a few seconds a year. Even if such states exist, their moral sublimity is far from obvious.

One might consider defending the moral dichotomy between humans and nonhumans on the ground that humans have immortal souls and nonhumans lack such souls. This defense is rarely heard in academic settings, either because it would be quite unfashionable or (better) because of the understanding that it rests on religious doctrine that is in fact contradicted by other religious doctrine. I certainly do not believe that I have (or am) an incorporeal, separable, spiritual entity that will survive bodily death. Of course I could be wrong. But every plausible reason I have to believe (or to doubt) that I have such a soul is also a reason to believe (or to doubt) that the dog barking across the street has one as well.

In fact, if it were true that humans have immortal souls and nonhumans lack them, that would not provide any reason to give priority to human interests. It would, rather, support assigning priority to the interests of nonhumans. Suppose one of the usual underdescribed imaginary cases. A building containing me and a turtle is on fire. You can only rescue one of us. Clearly, on this assumed distribution of souls, you should save the turtle. I can always be compensated later, but the turtle only goes around once.

The strongest arguments for the moral dichotomy are those of the contractarians and their kin. Morality is a matter of agreement, of (actual or hypothetical) contract. The contract governs and applies only to contractors. Those who cannot make agreements are therefore beyond the bounds of morality. As Alexandra puts it, the classes of moral agents (those whose behavior can be evaluated morally) and of moral patients (those the treatment of which is morally significant) are identical.

Broadly contractarian thinking is pervasive in economics, politics, and philosophy at the turn of the twenty-first century, but again and again it is challenged for excluding vulnerable beings from consideration. Nonhumans (at least most of them) are incapable of making or understanding agreements, but so are infants, the severely intellectually impaired, the very senile, and the dead—but all of these typically have legal standing, and it is widely believed that they have moral standing as well.

Species Overlap

In regard to every plausible candidate characteristic for moral status, either some humans lack that characteristic or the distribution of the characteristic overlaps species boundaries. That is, whatever property it may be that constitutes the ticket for admission to the moral community, either some humans will be excluded or some nonhumans will be included, or both. Most nonhumans cannot make agreements (at least with us), so the contractarian excludes them. Are the humans who cannot make agreements also to be excluded? Some contractarians will bite this bullet, but few chew on it in public.

The problem for most such thinkers, then, is how to bring noncontracting humans (infants, etc.) into the tent without admitting either the camel or his nose. One family of proposed solutions to this problem brings in these "other" humans on the coattails of normal adult humans—the paradigm contractors.

In *A Theory of Justice* Rawls stipulates that his hypothetical contractors know that they will be human and must act as heads of families.[4] But both stipulations seem simply arbitrary. Further, a head of family might well be taken as head of a household containing multiple species.

A similar move grants derivative standing to infants, etc. on the ground that (some? many? surely not all) paradigm contractors care deeply about them. It is obviously correct that many contracting adults do concern themselves with the welfare of infants, children, the severely impaired, and the senile, and even with the interests of the dead. And it is equally obvious that contracting adults are concerned with the welfare of nonhuman animals, the preservation of species and mountains, the protection of ancient artifacts, and the maintenance of Elvis memorabilia.

Clearly these moves won't work. If noncontracting humans are to be promoted to full moral status, it will have to be on some property or properties they possess, not the attitudes of privileged beings.

One attempt of this sort goes as follows. Infants, young children, the seriously impaired, and the hopelessly demented are all humans. Typical, standard, human adults have the status-granting properties (ability to contract or whatever). Therefore, as members of a class whose members typically qualify for full moral status, infants, young children, etc. qualify for full moral status. The implied principle is that all members of a class whose typical members have qualifying attributes (whatever those are) ipso facto must be taken as having those attributes. This, however, is just silly. Adult humans in prosperous countries typically are qualified for driver's licenses. Given that I am an adult human in a prosperous country, do I automatically get a driver's license? Perhaps I am blind, or totally untrained or just incompetent. This dodge is just speciesism in the lightest of disguises.

More sophisticated, perhaps, is a potentiality argument. Human infants and small children (and fetuses) are not capable of making or understanding contracts. But they have the potentiality of developing into creatures that are so capable. So they should be granted at least provisional full moral status. To give this argument its full weight, we must distinguish between mere possibility and a stronger notion of potentiality. This kind of potentiality consists in being somewhere along a path of development that, if all goes well, leads to the privileged end state.

Contractarians who take this route still have some bullets to bite. Some infants and children (and adults) do not in fact possess such potential. They will never develop in the "standard" way. The terminally demented may once have had the potential, may once in fact have been full-fledged contractors, but they are no more, and will not be again. These humans, members of the species *Homo sapiens*, must be excluded from the garden.

But the potentiality argument doesn't really work even for normal infants and children. The underlying principle, that an entity at an early point in some progression that leads to status X should therefore be accorded status X, is unacceptable. We are all potential cadavers, or, once we purchase a lottery ticket, potential millionaires. It certainly does not follow that we should be treated as cadavers, or as millionaires.

Here is a better analogy: many years ago I was appointed a midshipman. I was thus a potential admiral. The percentage of midshipmen who become admirals is quite small, but it is much greater than the percentage of those who have never been midshipman who become admirals. A few years later I was commissioned an ensign, thus moving along the pathway of potentiality, with an increased probability of ending as an admiral. In due course I was promoted to lieutenant junior grade, to lieutenant, to lieutenant commander, to commander, and, twenty-five years after becoming a midshipman, to captain. Only one step remained, but I did not take it. I retired as a captain. I never became an admiral, even though I was certainly a potential admiral. Obviously, as a potential admiral, I was not entitled to an admiral's pay or an admiral's flag, or to style myself an admiral. A potential X, no matter how strong the degree of potentiality, is just not ipso facto an X.

Perhaps the most central of Alexandra's arguments is that if one wishes to assign full moral status (human rights) to every single human, it can only be on the basis of morally significant properties shared by every human. Since the only such properties are the capacities for suffering and happiness, and these are shared by many, many nonhumans, universal human rights can only be universal rights for the sentient.

Hierarchy

It is possible to construct a coherent hierarchical theory of moral status, but it would still be vulnerable to the species overlap objection. In such a theory the status of each individual would be directly proportioned to the level of that individual's possession of the relevant properties (whatever they are: awareness, self-consciousness, etc.). However, this would entail that, since the level of self-consciousness of (for example) a newborn human is clearly below that of an adult dog, the newborn's moral standing would be lower than that of the dog. Although a really tough-minded contractarian might be willing to accept this, probably no actual hierarchical thinker would.

Almost all of us, in our ordinary lives and our day-to-day moral judgments, believe in moral hierarchy. Some things matter a lot, some less, some very little, and some not at all. But these practical hierarchies are almost universally muddled and conceptually incoherent. All humans rank above all animals (and thus our hierarchies are vulnerable to species overlap arguments), and some animals rank much higher than others, usually mammals and birds above reptiles and fish and all vertebrates above invertebrates. Value usually drops near zero for insects, and effectively never extends to microorganisms.

Our hierarchies are muddled in a number of ways. Some value the existence of (some) species above that of individuals, but it is hard to conceive of a morally significant property that could be possessed by an abstract object to a higher degree than by a sentient individual. Most of us rank cats and dogs and horses above cattle and swine, and those again above rats, but there is no property of intelligence or sentience that justifies such an ordering.

Even if a consistent hierarchy resting on intellectual complexity could be constructed, which would require a confidence in our judgments of such complexity that cannot now be justified, it is not clear that it could be defended. First, we really do not know how complex the experience and understanding of other animals may be. We are very, very far from a neuroscience that could make such determinations. In April 2007 a massive supercomputer with 4,096 powerful processors in parallel managed to simulate, at one-tenth speed, one half of the brain of a mouse for one second. And that was possible only with such simplifying assumptions as that all neuronal connections were initially random.

The mental life of many animals may be much more complex than we imagine. But, second, even if it isn't, even if animal minds are much simpler than ours, their happiness and suffering may be as important as ours. Suppose my cat and I both need dental surgery. Since we have essentially the same neurological pain system, let us stipulate that our pains are of the same level. (Of course we don't really have such measurements, but let's pretend.) Our sufferings, however, are quite different, and the cat suffers more than I do. I know that the dentist is not trying to hurt me. I understand the necessity for the procedure. I know that it will be over fairly soon. Finally, I can distract myself by making up stories or computing powers of two (which is what I actually do). The cat, we have assumed, has a much simpler mind. He does not know what is going on. He does not know that it will end, ever. He cannot distract himself as I can. He knows only that he is restrained and cannot escape and that he is in pain. I experience pain and discomfort. The cat experiences pain and sheer terror. You will not convince me that my suffering is worse than the cat's, nor in itself more important than the cat's.

Limits of Possibility

In principle ethics is impartial, but we certainly are not. It is not just that we are more concerned with those close to us in kinship or affection. Even when we have no personal connection with those who suffer misfortune, we are moved much more by some sufferers than by others.

A very striking illustration of this occurred in April 2007. A severely disturbed young man at Virginia Tech shot dozens of people, killing thirty-two of them. The reaction to these tragic deaths was extraordinary. The event was headline news around much of the world. The President of the United States came to Blacksburg, as did one of the largest concentrations of the electronic media the world has ever seen. In the United States there was nearly continuous coverage on all the major networks for several days (despite the fact that for most of that time there was really nothing to report). The Queen of England and the President of Ireland were among the notables expressing their condolences. The Virginia Tech shootings were in the Yahoo News top five news topics for two weeks.

In that same month more than 100 American and other coalition troops died in Iraq, and hundreds and hundreds of Iraqis. Those deaths (at least most of them) were tragic too, but much less notice was taken of them.

Statistical comparisons are even more striking. The 33 people (including the killer) who died on the Virginia Tech campus that day were $1/10$ of 1 percent of the university ($1/10$ of 1 percent of the faculty and staff and $1/10$ of 1 percent of the student body). They were $1/10$ of 1 percent of those killed by guns in the United States in 2007. More people died that day, in the United States, of inadequate health care, and many, many more in Africa of inadequate health care.

Why this bizarre disproportion? Of course the premature and surely undeserved deaths at Virginia Tech are tragic. But so are thousands of these others. For the families and friends and lovers of the killed, no justification is needed. For the distant, or even the fairly close with no personal connection, complete justification seems unlikely. (Among the fairly close, I count myself. I live in Blacksburg and taught for more than thirty years at Virginia Tech, several times in the very classrooms in which most of the murders took place.)

So why was there so much attention? It was a dramatic event, but no more so than that day's firefights in Baghdad. It was a surprise and a shattering of the peaceful and protected picture we have of universities, and of none more so than Virginia Tech in its rural mountain setting. Certainly it was in large part a product of media hype and the exploitation of fear. Perhaps there was a widespread feeling that it could have been us or been ours. If so, that says something unflattering about our collective imaginations, for it could have been us or ours in Iraq as well.

From the viewpoint of an impartial ethics, the problem is not that we cared too much about the Virginia Tech victims but that we cared too little about all the rest. Iraq and Afghanistan have become just the barely noted background of events. The Congo and Sri Lanka are even less detectable. And the human costs of profit-based medicine in America and grossly inadequate medicine in Africa are, for most of us most of the time, completely lost in the background noise.

The point of this lengthy digression is that our psychology constrains what we can reasonably expect of others or of ourselves. Even if our impartial theory persuades us that all suffering matters, it is just not within our powers to attend to all of it (or even very much of it). Some such limit is probably necessary in any case, for to be conscious of too much of the world's suffering would be unendurable. (There is an asymmetry here. It would also be impossible to be conscious of all the world's happiness. But no theory suggests that we should feel guilty about that.)

It seems to be effectively impossible for most of us to take the interests of nonhuman animals as seriously as those of humans. In my daily walks I often see squirrels who have been killed by cars. They sadden me, but not too much and not for very long. If I came upon a dead human in the road my reaction would be quite different. The deaths of the nonhumans just don't seem as important. But evaluating and explaining the harm of death is notoriously difficult, since some deaths do not seem to be harms at all, and in others it is hard to say who suffers any harm. The good of happiness and the bad of suffering are less obscure. Is human suffering worse than animal suffering? Is human happiness better?

We do in fact almost all believe that human interests are more important than nonhuman interests. But there is no sound argument to support this belief. The belief may well be a self-deception. Collectively we used to believe that the interests of our race, our nation, or our class were weightier than those of other human groups. Such beliefs are certainly not extinct. We can easily imagine a Roman slaveholder for whom the interests of his pet animals are more important than those of his human slaves. For anyone in the least likely to be reading this, however, the belief, almost certainly, is that human interests trump nonhuman interests. This may be a delusion. But, for the sake of argument, let us assume that some form of this belief is ineliminable.

That is certainly not to say that any human interest is more important than any nonhuman interest. We believe in hierarchy, not dichotomy. Human interests are more important, but animal interests matter. Human interests outrank nonhuman interests *ceteris paribus*. Just when *ceteris* are *paribus* usually cannot be determined with any precision. Even with such quantifiable goods as money we often cannot rank interests. If we know the current assets, preferences, and history of Sam and Sally, it still may be impossible to determine if $100 presented to Sam produces more, less, or an equal amount of happiness as $100 presented to Sally.

Fortunately, precision is rarely needed. We can distinguish, roughly but often quite definitely, between minor interests and major interests. If I come upon you just after a serious accident, it is obvious that your interest in not bleeding to death is more significant than my interest in not getting my clothes bloody. My interest in renting a movie is trivial in comparison to the interest of a refugee in Darfur in keeping her child alive, even if I usually succeed in not thinking about the comparison.

So, even if major human interests take priority over major nonhuman interests, and trivial human interests take priority over trivial nonhuman interests, still major interests of nonhuman animals may well outrank trivial interests of humans. In fact, all of us who are not dichotomists already believe this, albeit in a very weak form. We condemn deliberate cruelty despite the fact that it gives a human pleasure. In a clearer case, it would be outrageous for a human to condemn a dozen monkeys to hours of torture just to spare herself ten minutes of headache.

A Very Simple Principle

Happiness and suffering matter, no matter what the identity or species of the happy or suffering being. A simple (in principle) form of hedonistic consequentialism, called utilitarianism by philosophers, holds that in the end nothing else matters. But one need not be a utilitarian or a consequentialist of any sort to agree that happiness and suffering matter. Strip the claim down even further: suffering is bad. What results is a very minimal principle of behavior: do not act in ways that cause unnecessary suffering. One may well have other principles, and rules or heuristics dealing with the interactions of principles, but this you must have: do not act in ways that cause unnecessary suffering.

Conflict and Convenience

When, at small cost to myself, I can avoid causing animal suffering, the principle requires that I do so. Since all fur production involves severe animal suffering and death, and the choice of fur (for 99.99 percent of humans) is simply a matter of satisfying intrinsically trivial desires, it follows that one should not buy or wear fur. Since there is no nutritional need for humans to eat animal flesh, preferences of taste are inherently minor, and almost all contemporary animal agriculture entails massive suffering, we should all be vegetarians.

When minor interests of humans and animals conflict, our principle allows giving precedence to the humans. My interest in growing tulips and hostas conflicts with the interest of the neighborhood deer in eating those delicacies. My interest in feeding birds conflicts with a clever raccoon's interest in emptying my feeders. I am justified in chasing away the deer and raccoons and in trying to protect plants and feeders, but not in killing or seriously harming the animals.

Serious conflicts of interest between humans and nonhumans are actually quite rare in the lives of most of us. If I am attacked by a bear or alligator I can rightly defend myself with fatal force if necessary, just as if I were attacked by another human.

Concentration on glum and frightful remote possibilities should not prevent us from seeing that decreasing the amount of animal suffering for which we are responsible is actually quite easy. It is sometimes mildly inconvenient to be a vegetarian, but only mildly. It is a bit more difficult to be a vegan. As more and more people make these choices, they will become less inconvenient. For most of us, a gradual slide into vegetarianism is in fact quite pleasant.

In addition to the reduction of suffering, there are other bonuses. Vegetarian diets are healthy, and if all or most of us gave up meat the whole human world could be fed using much less land, and environmental degradation would appreciably slow.[5] Animal agriculture, from the feedlots and pig factories of the developed world to the sheep and goats that keep the Sahara growing southward, is one of the most destructive forces on the planet.

So come on, Theo. It's not hard to get started. No flesh for dinner tonight.

Toward an Agnostic Animal Ethics

MATTHEW CALARCO

THERE ARE A number of things about Paola Cavalieri's writings[1] that I admire and with which I am in near complete agreement. I want to begin here by briefly articulating these points. I do so, however, not with the aim of developing a kind of *homoiōsis* between our respective positions, but rather in order to elaborate more precisely where my approach to animal ethics, which is informed by recent work in both analytic and continental philosophy, differs from hers; and create the space within which a critical exchange about the larger stakes of animal ethics can occur.

Like Cavalieri, I find perfectionist theories of moral status to be philosophically untenable and ethically and politically pernicious. The arguments presented throughout "The Death of the Animal: A Dialogue on Perfectionism" constitute, to my mind, a welcome and formidable addition to existing arguments against perfectionism in animal ethics,[2] and they provide further reasons for the rejection of the kind of inegalitarian and hierarchical position associated with such authors as Baruch Brody, who argue that moral partialism relieves us of strong moral duties toward animals.[3] Consequently, I concur with the dialogue's overarching thesis, which I take to be that perfectionism is a concept that can and should be eliminated from contemporary ethical discourse.

A corollary of this thesis in Cavalieri's dialogue concerns the concept of "the animal," which she (or rather, the character of Alexandra Warnock) suggests must also be eliminated if actual animals are to be treated with full and fair moral consideration. Her assumption here is that "the animal" is situated at the bottom of a classical moral hierarchy in which paradigm human beings are situated at the top. It is only by challenging this placement of "the animal," along with the hierarchical logic that constitutes the implicit backdrop of debates over the moral status of animals, that the established order can be overturned. I am in full agreement with this corollary as well.

There are other arguments that could be made on behalf of the rejection of perfectionism in theories of moral status and for the dissolution of the concept of the animal. But rather than presenting these additional arguments concerning points on which Cavalieri and I are largely in agreement, I should like to engage her work more critically and examine two aspects of her position on animal ethics that I find less tenable: her negative characterization of the metaphysical character of continental philosophy and her specific approach to the question of moral status. After addressing these two issues, I present a version of animal ethics inspired by Emmanuel Levinas that avoids some of the problems I point out in Cavalieri's project.

Continental Philosophy and the Autonomy of Ethics

Throughout "The Death of the Animal," and in several of her other writings, Cavalieri is intent on establishing the inability of contemporary continental philosophy to address and contest the ethical and political status quo of animals in modern societies. In my own work, I have arrived at a different, and more positive, conclusion regarding the continental tradition's relation to "the question of the animal"; and I assume that by being asked to participate in this dialogue, along with a novelist and an analytic philosopher, I am to serve as a sort of representative of that tradition and respond to the charge being leveled against it. Given the richness and variability inherent in the continental tradition, and given that the term "continental philosophy" is for me little more than a family resemblance concept that gathers together a broad range of thinkers and texts, I will neither presume to represent it nor try to salvage the tradition as a whole by suggesting that continental philosophy as such has more or better resources for addressing the question of the animal. My aim in this section, rather, is briefly to address the criticisms that Cavalieri has made against the continental tradition and suggest that they seriously miss the mark.

In "The Death of the Animal," Alexandra attributes the possibility of developing a nonperfectionist animal ethics to two major changes in ethical discourse. The first change concerns the use of the analytic method of argumentation, and the second involves recognizing the autonomy of ethics as a distinct mode of inquiry. This latter notion is my concern here. Alexandra characterizes the autonomy of ethics as involving a view of ethics as a "theoretical inquiry endowed with its own standards of justification, within which criteria coming from other domains—be they religious, metaphysical, or scientific—have no direct relevance." Cavalieri herself makes this same point about the autonomy of ethics in several places,[4] and she is keen to stress that an animal ethics can only be egalitarian when divorced from the idiosyncratic worldviews that have governed Western metaphysics. Cavalieri's point here is that most traditional metaphysical worldviews have been uncritically hierarchical and anthropocentric; and when ethics is subordinated to metaphysics, ethics itself becomes similarly hierarchical and anthropocentric. In severing ethics from metaphysics, Cavalieri believes that ethics can then approach the question of moral status in a more impartial, less metaphysical manner.

Following Mary Warnock, Cavalieri suggests in *The Animal Question* that continental philosophy has been unable to make this turn and still subordinates ethical discourse to metaphysics.[5] As a result, continental philosophy ends up providing little more than a recapitulation of the hierarchical and anthropocentric ethics that form the status quo of Western metaphysics.[6] I find this criticism to be deeply uncharitable and inaccurate, inasmuch as nearly all of the major continental philosophers she discusses in her work (which include Friedrich Nietzsche, Martin Heidegger, and Jacques Derrida) do *not* subordinate ethics to metaphysics (in many cases, precisely the opposite is the case)[7] or subscribe to a hierarchical and anthropocentric ethics (at least not in any straightforward manner). These are enormously complex philosophical issues, and there is no possibility of adequately addressing them in the space that I have at my disposal. But I will say very briefly that what motivates the work of all of the thinkers just mentioned is trying to contest Western metaphysics and create the possibility of developing a mode of thought and practice that does not fall back squarely within the conceptual and practical constraints of the metaphysical tradition; and if none of these thinkers ends up subscribing to the discourse of rights and its implicit presuppositions, it is not (as Cavalieri seems to suggest) because their thinking is uncritically metaphysical or anthropocentric. Rather, they all approach ethics and the question of the animal outside the framework of rights because they believe (and rightly so, in my opinion) that *rights discourse and its axioms are themselves metaphysical*.[8]

The Question of Moral Status

One of the main ways rights discourse is metaphysical can be seen more clearly by examining how the debate over moral status functions in the human rights/animal rights version of moral theory defended by Cavalieri. She has the character of Alexandra pose the question of moral status at the very beginning of "The Death of the Animal," in view of the lack of understanding of this concept from Theo Glucksman, the other main participant in the dialogue (who is, notably, trained as a continental philosopher). After remarking on the significant differences between the analytic and continental traditions on this issue, Alexandra explains the concept of moral status in the following terms: "One's moral status is one's place in the moral community: how much does one count? To what degree are one's interests protected? As you can see, questions of moral status lie at the very core of ethics."[9]

Cavalieri examines the concept of moral status in her own voice in *The Animal Question*, where she highlights its two main functions:

> On one side, the notion [of moral status] performs the fundamental function of pointing out that the arrangement of the different entities within the moral community should be categorized in specifically ethical terms. On the other, however, it can be more generically employed to shed light on specific answers to the question of which beings other than the [moral] agent should have their interests protected, and to what degree.[10]

In brief, then, the concept of moral status serves to demarcate the kinds of beings to whom obligations are owed, that is, it delimits the scope of moral patients as well as what kinds of obligations are owed to them.

As I have already mentioned, I am largely in agreement with Cavalieri's critique of perfectionist theories that seek to determine moral status in hierarchical and inegalitarian ways. Her work is extraordinarily effective in showing how the kinds of hierarchies and inequalities that plague the rights tradition are inconsistent with the fundamental axioms and premises of that tradition. And to the extent that her arguments are understood as having a *dialectical* rather than *demonstrative* status within that tradition,[11] I find her project to be progressive and distinctly nonmetaphysical. The problem that I have with Cavalieri's approach arises when these positive dialectical arguments in favor of expanding the inclusive scope of rights and moral status are used negatively to exclude and restrict other entities from those protections.

Like nearly every philosopher working in analytic animal ethics, Cavalieri seeks to determine the criterion or criteria that cleanly demarcates those beings who belong to the community of moral patients from those beings who do not. While this gesture appears perfectly rational within the supposedly "autonomous" discourse of contemporary analytic ethics, the very idea strikes me as deeply metaphysical and subordinated to traditional metaphysical ends. As so many continental philosophers have pointed out (among them Friedrich Nietzsche, Martin Heidegger, Emmanuel Levinas, Theodor Adorno, Jacques Derrida, and Giorgio Agamben), the effort to determine who does and does not belong to the moral community is one of the most problematic foundational gestures in the Western metaphysical tradition and is indicative of its imperialistic tendencies.[12]

Thus, before rushing to determine a new line of demarcation that excludes a new and different class of entities from moral consideration, perhaps we who are interested in animal ethics should pause to examine the implicit presuppositions of this entire project. Why do we need to determine the outer limits of moral status beyond animals? What if the logic of deciding inclusion and exclusion within the moral community were itself the problem? And what would be the implications for ethics if we were to abandon the aim of determining the proper limits of moral status altogether?

Agnostic Ethics

One of the leading continental ethical philosophers, Emmanuel Levinas, provides an alternative way of understanding ethics that can be used to overcome the kinds of implicit metaphysical presuppositions at work in Cavalieri's discourse and much of contemporary analytic animal ethics. Following Levinas, ethics can be generally defined as an interruption of my egoism coming from the face of an Other that transforms my being in the direction of generosity. In other words, ethics combines responsivity to the face with an enacted responsibility. Levinas's most common examples are typically focused on the way the Other's destitution and vulnerability call my spontaneity into question and lead me to give up my possessions in order to ameliorate the Other's suffering. In his later writings, Levinas increasingly describes ethics in terms of my being called to be with the Other in the face of the Other's death. But in both cases, the formal structure of ethics remains the same: it involves a disruption of my perseverance in being that deeply affects and transforms my entire existence such that the Other becomes my priority.

There is, of course, no reason to believe that ethics as such is *exhausted* by the specific kinds of encounters Levinas privileges. There are any number of ways my egoism might be interrupted, any number of kinds of entities that might disrupt me, and any number of ways I might be transformed by such encounters—several of which could just as suitably be called "ethical" as the ones Levinas highlights. So, what would ethics look like if we took seriously Levinas's definition but didn't limit ourselves to the precise kinds of ethical encounters he emphasizes? Simply put, ethics would become rigorously and generously *agnostic*. But what exactly does this mean? If we distinguish among the ways my egoism might be interrupted, the kinds of entities who might call me into question, and the manner in which such interruptions might transform me, it is clear that the central issue concerning ethical agnosticism revolves around the second point: the kinds of entities who might call me into question. In other words, it concerns the limits of moral status.

With regard to the question of *who* might interrupt me, that is, to whom I might find myself obligated and to whom moral status should be granted—here too I think a rigorous and generous agnosticism is called for. But this is a difficult pill for many people to swallow. For surely the Other (whom Levinas typically delimits to the human other) cannot be infinite in this sense, without any definable limits a priori, and capable of taking any form. But if it is indeed the case, as Levinas suggests, that ethics arises from an encounter with an Other who is fundamentally irreducible to and unanticipatable by my egoistic and cognitive machinations, and if it is indeed the case that we cannot know in advance where the face begins and ends, where moral status begins and ends, then we are obliged to proceed from the possibility that *anything* might take on a face. And we are further obliged to hold this possibility permanently open.

At this point, I suspect that most analytically inclined animal ethicists (Cavalieri included) will see the argument I am making as having absurd consequences. While it might not be unreasonable to consider the possibility that animals who are subjects (which is where Cavalieri draws the line of moral consideration) could have a moral claim on us, are we also to believe that animals without any sort of subjectivity, as well as insects, dirt, hair, fingernails, ecosystems, and so on could also have a claim on us? Any argument that leads to this possibility is surely a *reductio ad absurdum*. At the very least, it *must* be based on an outmoded metaphysics, the critic might suggest.

I should like to ask the critic in turn: is it at all reasonable to conclude that there is a genuinely rational or objective way to determine the limits of moral status? And does not a historical survey of the failures that have attended every such attempt to draw *the* line (or lines) of moral considerability provide enough evidence to persuade common-sense moral discourse that this approach is inherently pernicious, both morally and politically?

From Moral Status to Universal Consideration

Thomas Birch makes a similar set of points about the problematic aspects of the moral status debate in his essay, "Moral Considerability and Universal Consideration."[13] He notes that from a "historical perspective, we see that whenever we have closed off the question [of moral considerability] with the institution of some practical criterion, we have later found ourselves in error, and have had to open the question up again to reform our practices in a further attempt to make them ethical."[14] The lesson that Birch draws from this historical perspective parallels the point I have been making thus far: the question of who the Other is, that is, of who might make a claim on me and thus be morally considerable, cannot be determined with any finality. Unless we proceed from this kind of generous agnosticism, not only are we bound to make mistakes (who would be bold enough to claim that rationality or descriptive phenomenology will overcome our finitude and specific historical location in making such judgments?), but also we set up the conditions of possibility for the worst kinds of abuses toward those beings who are left outside the scope of moral concern.

As Birch explains, the main problem with much of moral theory and practice is that it is premised on the belief that there *should* be an inside and outside with regard to moral considerability. Moral theory and practice has

> presupposed (1) that when it comes to moral considerability, there *are*, and *ought* to be, insiders and outsiders, citizens and non-citizens (for examples, slaves, barbarians, and women), "members of the club" of *consideranda* versus the rest; (2) that we *can* and *ought* to identify the mark, or marks, of membership; (3) that we *can* identify them in a rational and non-arbitrary fashion; and (4) that we *ought* to institute practices that enforce the marks of membership and the integrity of the club, as well, of course, as maximizing the good of its members.[15]

That these presuppositions betray a rather unethical, even imperialistic starting point, coupled with the fact that they have served as the ground for some of the worst atrocities human beings have committed, should be enough to make us rethink this approach to ethics from the ground up. Furthermore, it is not at all clear that ethical *experience* permits such neat and tidy divisions of who does and does not count, of where my concern should begin and end, and of who has a face and who does not. And is this not the chief lesson of Levinas's thought? If we are to learn anything from Levinas, it is that ethical experience occurs precisely where phenomenology and rationality is interrupted, and that ethical experience is traumatic, radically disruptive, and not easily captured by thought. Given its diachronic structure, it can at best be only partly reconstructed in thetic form. This would, it seems, require us always to proceed agnostically and generously, as if we might have missed or misinterpreted the Other's trace.

Rather than trying to determine the definitive criterion or criteria of moral considerability, we might, following Birch and the reading of Levinas I have been pursuing here, begin from a notion of "universal consideration" that takes seriously our fallibility in determining where the face and moral status begin and end. Universal consideration would entail being ethically attentive and open to the possibility that anything might take on a face; it would also entail taking up a skeptical and critical relation to the determinations of moral consideration that form the contours of our present moral thinking. Universal consideration is, as Birch suggests, a matter of "giving others of all sorts a chance to reveal their value, and of giving ourselves a chance to see it, rather than approaching them in hostility as if they have nothing but negative value until they have proved otherwise."[16]

It is important to stress that this notion of universal consideration does not make the positive claim that all things or all life forms *do* count; nor does it supply any positive claim concerning *how* various beings or relational structures might count. On both points, an ethics of universal consideration requires us to keep the question wide open.

☼ ☼ ☼

Now, if such caution is in fact required, then the question that arises is: why am I discussing *animal* ethics at all? Is this term not just as problematic as other classical limits, such as "the human"? And why limit the discussion just to animals? Why not cast the net wider? Or, if we take the notion of universal consideration seriously, why *name* the Other at all? The brief answer, and one that I will try to explain and defend here, is that it is necessary to take such risks. Contemporary ethical discourse and practice do not take place in a vacuum, but emerge from out of a series of background practices and beliefs that have placed the interests of most animals outside the scope of moral and political considerability. In order to challenge the established order of things in this context, it is necessary to take up the terms of the discourse as they currently stand and transform them. There are, then, several different reasons for focusing on the question of the animal in particular:

1. *The strategic disruption of metaphysical anthropocentrism.* One of the chief limitations for thought at present is "metaphysical anthropocentrism," or the tendency to determine nonhuman life in an oppositional and hierarchical manner with respect to the human. Nowhere is this problem more evident than in our thinking on the human-animal distinction. This site, perhaps more than any other (for example, human-machine, human-divine, human-environment, and so on), is the source of massive anxiety, inasmuch as our increasing knowledge of and familiarity with animals threatens not just to blur but even to eliminate this distinction altogether. As anthropocentrism with respect to animals becomes ever less tenable, anthropocentrism of other sorts is also called into question. In this sense, the animal question is one of the primary sites that must be passed through on the way toward another thought of human and nonhuman life, which will perhaps do away with or be unconcerned to think in terms of "the human" and its "others."

2. *The alterity of animals.* Philosophical discourse on animals has been overwhelmingly reductionistic and essentialist in its approach. Animals have often been thought of by philosophers as belonging to a single class of beings that lack some essential human trait (language, a concept of death, moral agency, and so on). As Jacques Derrida argues, not only does this approach gloss over the enormous differences that exist among animals themselves, it also offers a false characterization of the (nonessential) differences between human beings and animals (there is no single, insuperable dividing line).[17] To focus carefully on the ethical aspects of our interactions with animals forces us to return to this issue with more care than philosophers have traditionally taken. In so doing, we are confronted with the singularity and alterity of animals, with the fact that the beings we call animals do not fit into the categories under which we have placed them. It is because we do not know what animals can do (empirically) or what they might become (ontologically) that they exceed our conceptualization. And it is precisely in the breakdown of this process of conceptualization that their alterity comes to the fore.

3. Reconfiguring the link between the animal question and environmental issues. Historically, animal ethicists (Cavalieri included) have set themselves at odds with proponents of other forms of ethics that move beyond the human, and particularly with environmental ethics. Animal ethicists have, by and large, presented themselves as individualists, whereas the dominant forms of environmental ethics have taken a holistic or relational approach, with each camp pointing out the other's limitations. This difference has led to sharp divisions in both theory and practice. If, however, we address the question of animal ethics from the neo-Levinasian approach developed here, then such divisions get recast in a very different light. Animal ethics becomes but one way among others of thinking through ethics, with specific attention given to the manner in which various animals might have a claim on us and what consequences follow from responding to such claims. That other kinds of beings, systems, or relational structures might have a claim on us is not ruled out but rather is allowed in principle under an ethics of universal consideration. Thus, rather than being in opposition to each other, animal ethics and environmental ethics would be seen as two distinct but complementary forms of ethical inquiry and practice that seek to challenge the limits of anthropocentrism.

4. The lives and deaths of animals themselves. Perhaps it goes without saying, but it should nevertheless be stressed, that the animal question is particularly pressing given the present conditions under which many animals exist. Never before in human history have so many animals been subjected to horrific slaughter, unconscionable abuse, and unthinkable living conditions. These conditions have a unique history that requires both material and philosophical analysis; and it is a history that needs to be attended to in its *specificity* so that we might learn better how to transform it for the present and the future. Certainly, this does not mean that the history of the subjection of animals should not be thought alongside the history of other, interrelated forms of oppression, examples of which we find in the writings of ecofeminists and other progressive animal rights theorists.[18] The approach offered here should be seen as proceeding in the same spirit as and in deep solidarity with these approaches. But I also wish to underscore that the animal question cannot be fully reduced to or made identical with other human struggles against oppression. The logics of domination overlap at points, but they also diverge—and both the convergences and the divergences are equally important for thought and practice. Likewise, we need to pay specific attention to the unique ways animals themselves resist subjection and domination, even if their efforts are not wholly successful. The elephant who escapes from its imprisonment at a circus; the pig who flees the slaughterhouse and runs free in the streets until shot by police; the whales who protect each other from being shot with harpoons; the lion who mauls its human handler; the chimpanzee who attacks an experimental scientist; the feral cat who refuses to be handled—these and other such figures of animal resistance should remain at the core of animal ethics as much as the suffering animals whose terrible fate we indirectly catch sight of at mealtime or in underground videos of slaughterhouses.

✦ ✦ ✦

So, the approach to animal ethics I have outlined here differs from the standard analytic approaches in not seeing itself as developing *the* criterion or criteria by which something takes on a face or has moral status. Rather, animal ethics is seen here as a *risk*, a "fine risk" of the sort Levinas speaks of in *Otherwise Than Being or Beyond Essence*. It is a risk to focus on animals, even when this focus is open-ended and generously agnostic. It is a risk to constrain our thinking to focus on the specific history of animal subjection and resistance, even when that history is viewed in conjunction with other histories of struggle and oppression. There are no guarantees that we have gotten things right here, or that this particular approach will in fact have the kind of transformative effect we might desire. But such risks are what constitute the act of doing philosophy. They are fine risks, risks taken in the name of "the Other animal" and without any pretense of fully representing or understanding those singular beings we call animals.

Comments on Paola Cavalieri, "A Dialogue on Perfectionism"

JOHN M. COETZEE

LET US REFLECT on Alexandra and Theodore, the two interlocutors in this dialogue, and on the form of their exchange.

A and T are children of Socrates, not only in the way in which they speak but also in the relationship they have with each other. Whatever may go on between them once they have stepped off the page, on the page they exhibit an amicability of a rather bloodless and certainly sexless nature. They speak fluently, at times eloquently, but never with heat.

Their inhuman calm, which is of a piece with their unvarying rationality, is accompanied by an inhuman moderation of appetite. They consume (in moderate quantities) wine and nuts, but only (one feels) because ichor is not available in the Mediterranean resort where they meet.

A and T appear to have transcended those passions and appetites that we might call animal or, equally well, human. In their calm they are more than inhuman—they have become superhuman, godlike.

It is hard not to take the cool rationality that they practice—it would seem in all respects—as an affirmation of and advertisement for the life of reason.

QUESTION: To whom is the lifestyle, and perhaps even the life, of A and T available? Is it available to a horse?

ANSWER (*PACE* JONATHAN SWIFT): No, not as far as we know.

QUESTION: Is it available to human beings to whom grants to travel to philosophy conferences on islands in the Mediterranean are not an option?

ANSWER: In theory yes, but in practice no—it is confined to the upper intelligentsia.

QUESTION: Is it compatible with a life, off the page, devoted to brawling and guzzling and fucking?

ANSWER: Perhaps, but only with a measure of psychic dislocation.

CONCLUSION: It is hard not to take this dialogue as an affirmation of a life of reason as a higher life, higher than a life of passion and appetite, but also higher than the life of beings to whom flights of reason are unavailable and perhaps even impossible.

QUESTION: Is this dialogue not then an instance of perfectionism in practice?

There are people (not many professional philosophers among them) to whom brawling and guzzling and fucking represent, if not the highest activities in life, the activities during whose performance they feel most themselves—the activities that allow them to live out their being-in-the-world most fully. Such people tend to think that folk who meet on Mediterranean islands to savor a fleshless cuisine and have lengthy verbal exchanges about the nature of the good and the true, and who then retire to sleep in nunlike seclusion, are missing something—missing the best of life. Such folk find it easy to advocate rights for animals, they say, because they have no animal life themselves. They know nothing of the pleasures of life, of which the pleasure of stalking and slaying a beast less cunning and less strong than oneself, and cutting it up and cooking and eating it afterward, is, they say, one of the highest, though the pleasure of eating the well-cooked muscle flesh of an animal slaughtered by someone else is not to be dismissed.

It is not hard, such people say, to convince folk who are committed in their professional life to the elevation of the life of the mind over the life of the body that the passions and the appetites are negligible. It is harder to persuade people like us, to whom the so-called lower pleasures, the pleasures of the body, are the center of our lives.

II

Notes on Issues Raised by Matthew Calarco

JOHN M. COETZEE

One

We (participants in this dialogue) are where we are today not because once upon a time we read a book that convinced us that there was a flaw in the thinking underlying the way that we, collectively, treat nonhuman animals, but because in each of us there took place something like a conversion experience, which, being educated people who place a premium on rationality, we then proceeded to seek backing for in the writings of thinkers and philosophers.

Our conversion experience as often as not centered on some other mute appeal of the kind that Levinas calls the look, in which the existential autonomy of the Other became irrefutable—irrefutable by any means, including rational argument.

One role that philosophers can play in the present climate of concern about our relations with other animals is as providers of the kind of reasoned backing I have referred to. An equally important role might be to alert people to the phenomenon of the look, the appeal that might come at any moment in their lives.

Professional philosophers are drawn to the first role because there seems to be a positive need for their skills in the drafting of new laws governing the treatment of animals. They are attracted by the image of themselves as legislators. But there is an equally venerable image of the philosopher as a moral guide.

Two

The question: If certain beings other than human beings ought to have the protection of the law, or alternatively, if certain beings other than human beings may legitimately be said to make ethical demands on us, are there limits—for example, species limits—on what such beings may be?

In response, an anecdote. I have a car that stands in my garage, occupying space. Though in working order, it cannot be licensed because its chassis is too rusty. The rational course of action would be to have it removed—hauled away by a scrap merchant. This is something I find I cannot (i.e., will not) do. The car served me well for many years. I cannot treat it like junk. I cannot betray it.

I am not the only person in the world who behaves in this irrational way. Many people refuse to trash old clothes that have served them well. Instead they look for a new home for them (rationalizing this as finding someone else who will be prepared to wear them).

Is this kind of behavior to be admired? From an ethical point of view, it seems to me consistent with the attitude that friends (i.e., human friends), once made, cannot simply be discarded; furthermore, that friendship is rarely governed by reason. One does not choose one's friends according to rules. Becoming friends is like falling in love: one follows one's heart.

But of course, accumulating junk is not good for the economy of the individual life. It may be good to be able to make affective ties—with other human beings, with nonhuman animals, even with inanimate objects—but it is also good (in another sense) to be able to cut such ties when necessary. Being able to cut ties when necessity so demands may even entail a mature, "philosophical," recognition that this is and will always be a less than perfect world.

These remarks are relevant to our subject in the following way. As a result of actions that human beings took in the remote past, some species of animals (hereafter, for the sake of simplicity, called slave species) have become dependent on us. Simply stated, such slave species as sheep and cattle cannot survive in the world as it presently is without our care and assistance. We cannot treat such animals as we would treat old clothes, discarding them when we decide it is necessary (e.g., when we have all become vegetarians). We have, in effect, brought them into our world; we cannot conscientiously expect them to leave it, for there is nowhere else for them to go. For a while, or perhaps indefinitely, they will be junk from the past that we cannot get rid of.

Thus enters the question of human control over the sexual and reproductive lives of other species, a control that in the case of slave species is complete. I raise without further elaboration the question of whether the putative rights of animals ought not to include the right to an autonomous (i.e., unsupervised) sexual life and the right to parenthood "as God intended."

Pushing Things Forward

PAOLA CAVALIERI

I

The dialogue is the form rational ethics assumed when it first appeared in ancient Greece. Any attempt to reckon with our tradition should therefore start from this form, which, far from showing any need to be "completed," is a philosophical archetype. The dialogue is the son of the enigma—the "próblema" through which the god's hostility intrudes into the human sphere—and the father of discursive thinking—the agonistic encounter between reasoning individuals set in motion by a question in alternative form.[1] The art of dialectics, whose seeds can be traced back to pre-Sophistic eras, can plausibly be seen as the root of the appearance of logical thought in a world dominated by magical thinking.

In Plato's so-called aporetic dialogues—the earliest compositions that have an indeterminate conclusion and are considered closer to his master's teachings—the character of Socrates is probably more faithful to the real philosopher than in all later works. Here, in his exploration of the virtues, Socrates not only displays an exclusively ethical orientation, setting aside any other kind of study, but also shows that for him human knowledge is simply the ability to discuss from the point of view of one engaged in actually living, often in the workshops or in the market—just where he could find people who had not transcended "those passions and appetites that we might call animal or, equally well, human," in the words of John Coetzee. Only subsequently did Plato seek an ambitious philosophical grounding for Socrates' rationalist ambitions—one that made ethical discussion a matter for the initiated. With Plato's view that ethics cannot be isolated from a general understanding of the world, Socrates' discursive approach to ethics was replaced by global metaphysical perspectives. This was the founding gesture of our tradition—the one that has influenced all our moral philosophy through the ages. And, in contrast with many philosophical outlooks—most prominently the so-called hermeneutic one[2]—according to which one cannot legitimately speak about progress in the moral domain, one might call archaic the ethics that is still shaped by this perspective. Overloaded by general worldviews, based on values determined by an idiosyncratic conception of being, and prone to defend unwarranted hierarchies, such ethics made it difficult to see the simplicity of the problems, as well as of the solutions.

The challenge to perfectionism is to be seen against this background, which distorts and complicates any question. For how can one attack, e.g., the Aristotelian idea that the end of the free "man" is metaphysical contemplation while that of the slave is to please his master without first challenging Aristotle's idea of differences in nature? How can one criticize "man's" primacy within classic natural law theory without first undermining the view that human beings are the privileged fruit of creation, destined to play a special role in a community transcendentally regulated by God? Or how can one question the notion of the "special dignity" of human beings without first challenging the idea that nonrational beings are mere means, while rational beings are ends in themselves?

This insertion of foreign elements into moral philosophy has clear parallels in science. A renowned astronomer, for instance, has summarized the turns characterizing the history of astronomy among many other sciences.[3] The introduction of a priori philosophical or religious concepts to explain the natural world, he claims, checked the development of science, and of astronomy in particular, for more than a millennium. Already in the sixth century B.C., Pythagoras of Samos introduced the notion that nature can be described through numerical relations, and in the third century B.C. Aristarchus of Samos suggested that the Earth is a sphere revolving around the Sun, and that the stars seem to be fixed only because their distance from the Earth is so great. Copernicus knew all this through a passage from *The Sand Reckoner* by Archimedes, but officially rediscovered the heliocentric hypothesis about 1,800 years later—because, starting from Plato through Aristotle and the Christian theologians, astronomy, divorced from the natural world, had been dominated by metaphysical and religious approaches and concerns.

Science could proceed only by freeing itself from such external ties. The same holds for ethics. But this is not the only parallel between the two spheres. For in ethics too, before the rise of the attitude we have defined as archaic, there had been a different beginning. Just as before Plato, Greek science was inaugurating a promising approach and achieving important results, so Greek ethics was developing, with the Sophists and Socrates, a rational and autonomous method of inquiry. This original method, after being erased for centuries, has recently resumed its course, challenging what Friedrich Nietzsche called "the metaphysical befogging of everything true and simple—reason's struggle against reason."[4]

Reflecting on that process, as well as on the parallel processes in science, one might tentatively suggest that, when applied to some cultural contexts, the notion of "archaic" could operatively incorporate, alongside its *relative* chronological component referring to priority *with respect to something in question*, an *absolute* element having to do with such dichotomies as autonomy/heteronomy, homogeneity/heterogeneity, and clarity/obscurity. A slightly different way of stating this would be to say that, in the history of many disciplines, "archaism" has to do with something like what, borrowing from developmental psychoanalysis, can be defined as a "lack of differentiation"—both in an extradisciplinary and in an intradisciplinary sense. In this light, contemporary rational ethics in the analytic tradition can be said to have overcome archaism. For, very briefly, it is autonomous insofar as it does not depend on other domains, homogeneous insofar as it employs its specialized theoretical tools, and clear insofar as it is based on explicit argumentation.

As far as the issue of the moral treatment of nonhumans is concerned, the essay by Harlan B. Miller is a perfect instantiation of these qualities, and well exemplifies the kind of clarification of "everything true and simple" to which Friedrich Nietzsche referred. Miller clearly frames the problems in question, introduces basic principles, applies them to specific cases, meticulously and patiently dismantles contrary arguments, and then draws the conclusion of his line of reasoning. Moreover, his admirable mastery of the discourse allows him to remain limpid even in dealing with perspectives still dominated by "dogmatism and disdain for argument." Nothing can be more understandable than "simple consciousness of pain and pleasure matters. If pain were not aversive, it would not be pain and thus would serve no purpose (and there would be no mobile animals)." No attack on perfectionism can be simpler than "You will not convince me that my suffering is worse than the cat's, nor in itself more important than the cat's." Why, then, criticize and reject such an approach in the name of different views of ethics? Is it possible that the mermaids of posthumanist and continental ethics sing an old melody again?

II

Though Cary Wolfe's powerful discussion of the animal question in a posthumanist perspective gives a central role to the views of Jacques Derrida, it includes as well philosophers who inhabit other traditions, such as Stanley Cavell and Cora Diamond. Given the complexities of such a multiple-voices argument, it may be worth attempting a synthetic reconstruction. What, then, are the main points of Wolfe's criticism of analytic moral philosophy?

Central to such a criticism is the charge of neglecting two forms of passivity. The first is passivity to the ahuman technicity of language as a precondition of our subjectivity. On this view, in a Saussurian or semiological vein, since the subject must conform to the system of the rules of language as a system of differences, and since those differences, taking their meaning from their reciprocal relations, do not find their cause in the subject, there is always the possibility of deviation from the intended meaning. On the one hand, that possibility, by preventing language from being able to express "universals" that may uncover first principles in ethics, and, more generally, by ruling out any god's-eye standpoint, entails that justice is not reducible to the immanence of any juridico-political doctrine but is in an important sense impossible, so that at the roots of ethical responsibility is paradoxically its impossibility; and, on the other, by implying that we don't really have a concept of *the human*, it undermines the "picture of the human that is taken for granted in analytic philosophy," and allows for a reflection that enables us to come out of ourselves—to become *inhuman*.

The second form of passivity concerns instead physical embodiment, and revolves around the acknowledgment of the vulnerability and mortality that we share with nonhumans and that "forms the basis of our moral response to them." This passivity often manifests itself as an "exposure" to ethical experiences whose painful inexplicability may unseat our reason—something that undermines the approach to ethics based on the view that what is involved in moral thought is knowledge of empirical similarities and differences, and the testing and application of general principles. Indeed, in the face of the unsettling and panicking effect of such exposure, the return to moral debate, in which "the livingness and death of animals enter as facts that we treat as relevant in this or that way," can be seen as a sort of escape.

Wolfe's conclusion is that, without making room for these two forms of passivity, or even without wholly substituting them for the analytic, universalistic approach, ethics itself cannot but be reduced to the *antithesis* of ethics, and antispeciesism cannot but remain "humanist"— that is, cannot but reproduce a picture of the human that may foreclose the very project it pursues. What are we to make of all this?

Let's consider first the view that an ethical system based on universal principles is the antithesis of ethics, and that justice is "in an important sense impossible." To the idea that time is unreal, an author as devoid of metaphysical ambitions as G. E. Moore, one of the fathers of analytic moral philosophy, replied that he had had breakfast before he had had lunch.[5] Analogously, to the idea that general legal rules can never produce justice, one might answer with an apologue. In 1981, Jacques Derrida, after participating in a meeting of dissidents in Prague, was arrested by the Czechoslovakian police and put in jail. It was only after some days that he could be freed, thanks to an intervention by French President François Mitterrand, who appealed to the rule of law. In spite of any theoretical criticism of the generality of legal rules, Derrida could only receive justice thanks to the rule of law. Fully aware of the contradiction in which he was involved, the French philosopher created a new philosophical category where contradictory thoughts confront each other without intersecting—that of "the intellectual baroque."[6]

Ethics is too serious a matter to be subject to such maneuvers. Jacques Derrida was a human being, a French citizen, and a well-known philosopher, and he needed the protection of the rule of law to be saved. It is plausible to ask how animals—who are not members of the *Herrenspezies*, are not citizens of any state, have no names, and are mere items of property—can be saved without the help of a juridical framework. More generally, and more fundamentally: how can the weak—or the *Other*, as posthumanists prefer to say—be protected from the strong—or the *Self*—if, instead of framing a set of clear, universal, and impartial rules, one gets entangled in speculations within which the requirement of consistency tends to yield its supremacy, and urgent moral issues are seen as part of wider theoretical, ontological, and epistemological projects?

As far as the animal question is concerned, the results of such an overloaded approach fully testify to its inadequateness. For, though he compares our industrialized use of animals with "the worst cases of genocide" and defines the traditional notion of subjectivity as a sacrificial schema implying a "noncriminal putting to death" of animals,[7] Derrida simply erases the problem of the value of animal life by dismissing philosophical vegetarianism on the ground that, since when we introject corpses the operation is symbolic in the case of humans and both real and symbolic in the case of animals, the task of determining our responsibility is too "enormous" to be undertaken. All the more so: for Derrida, "the moral question is . . . not, nor has it ever been" whether one should or should not eat animals.[8] Unfortunately, this should come as no surprise in someone who states that it would be "asinine" (in French, *bête*, an adjective condensing idiocy and animality into a crassly anthropocentric expression) not to acknowledge the existence of an *abyssal rupture* between humans and animals (and in particular between us and those nonhuman great apes to whose attempted enfranchisement he turned a deaf ear) and who rejects any parallel between humans and nonhumans, even at the same mental level, as dangerous insofar as it is characterized by "geneticist" and "racial" attitudes.[9]

Had his approach to ethics been less undifferentiated, Derrida could have avoided many problems. For instance, he could have grasped the distinction between a descriptive recourse to science in relevant empirical matters, such as the possession by some beings of characteristics to which human egalitarianism has already granted moral weight (something that, being part of an *ad hominem* argument, does not in itself violate Hume's guillotine), and a normative use of biological categories, such as the direct introduction of membership in a genetic group as a morally relevant characteristic. Also, he could have understood that— quite apart from the ontological investigations of a philosopher such as Martin Heidegger, whose "complex relationship to Nazism" led him to attempt to "spiritualize" it (in Derrida's own words)[10]—what is really "sinister" is the inconsistency of rejecting the moral relevance of membership in a particular biological group such as race, while obstinately defending a moral barrier between humans and nonhumans that concretely issues in a blatant instance of biologistic discrimination based on species. Finally, he would have probably been less obsessed by "the human" and by "ethical responsibility." But, to deal with this last point, it is worth now returning to the second form of passivity, which concerns Cavell and Diamond as well.

At the core of the discourse on passivity as physical vulnerability lies in fact a double reference to being human and to being a responsible agent, for "exposure to the world" appears to imply a recognition of *human* vulnerability and hesitancy that generates in the *subject* a suitable response to an arena of moral complexity and a loving attention to other beings. Indeed, both aspects are even more marked in Cavell and Diamond than in Derrida. As for the obsession with "the human," Cavell, after reading vegetarianism not as the sparing of animal lives but as a shorthand to good conscience—thus taking for granted just that moral inferiority he wishes to prove—asserts that, to reminders of "the company we may keep with nonhuman animals," he simply answers (shouts?), "I am human";[11] and Diamond declares that we cannot determine any difference in treatment independently of seeing what *particular human sense* humans have actually made out of the involved differences or similarities.[12] As for the stress on moral agency, Cavell's notion of "perfectionism" is clearly connected not with moral status but with the old sense of the individual pursuit of excellence, and Diamond's interest in the agent's feelings of woundedness and compassion far outweighs in importance the actual treatment of the victims.

What is one to say of all this? To the emphasis on humans and "human sense," one might object that even a white racist could answer "I am white" to reminders of the company one may keep with nonwhites, and—with Stephen Clark[13]—that it is hazardous to entrust ethical conduct to the fortuitousness of a moral history that could have been even worse than it was had we been, e.g., an intelligent species not of primates but of supermantises. As for the stress on moral agents, whatever the credit one can give to the human capacity for empathy, why should the existence of "unsettling compassion" discredit the rational approach to ethics founded on the application of general principles? Why shouldn't it merely integrate this approach, by supplying, for instance, *pace* Kant, moral motivation?

Again, something seems to have gone wrong with this way of doing ethics. For only within a tradition marked by regret for the loss of "human essence" (le *propre de l'homme* [sic]) and by the centrality of the ingrained tradition of virtue ethics can such contradictions and distortions emerge. All in all, it seems that, despite their apparently critical attitudes, posthumanist philosophers still are, as Harlan Miller would say, "in the grip of a theory"—and the theory is, once again, a form of moral perfectionism based on the primacy of moral agents. In this light, it is now time to turn to moral patients.

III

Questions of moral status often arise when traditional views are challenged. Recent history has seen the continuous attempt to widen the privileged circle of moral equality, with a progression in granting basic protection to women, children, the mentally enfeebled, and racial minorities. In our case, the focus is instead nonhuman animals—though one cannot overemphasize the fact that perfectionism has jeopardized the moral status of many members of our species for most of our philosophical history, and it is only recently that, as Harlan Miller puts it, less cognitively endowed humans have been brought into the community of equals "on the coattails" of paradigmatic humans (a solution, by the way, that, as Miller aptly adds, clearly cannot work, since by evading the question of the moral relevance of cognitive makeup it leaves the former at the mercy of the latter).

How has this progression occurred in the case of humans? Clearly, through the ascription of fundamental rights. Unlike "natural rights," fundamental moral rights—whose lineage cannot be traced here—do not present themselves as ontologically grounded entities, but rather as creatures of ethical theory—and especially precious creatures, given that, as Richard Wasserstrom stresses in a famous essay on racial discrimination, their presence enhances the moral landscape just in that it makes it possible to focus on the beings who are adversely affected by the action, that is, on the beings who suffer the injury.[14] Why, then, should the other animals be deprived of this valuable resource—"one of [the] most fruitful and important critical concepts" of our normative systems?[15] Why should we suppose that the nonhumans who, as Matthew Calarco acutely notes, "resist subjection and domination even if their efforts are not wholly successful"—the elephant who escapes from her imprisonment at a circus, the pig who flees the slaughterhouse, the whales who protect each other, the lion who mauls his human handler, the chimpanzee who attacks an experimental scientist—wouldn't be more than ready to take profit of it?

And yet, in both Wolfe's and Calarco's discussion, we find an attack on the idea of granting rights to nonhumans. Wolfe approvingly quotes Derrida saying that "to confer or to recognize rights for 'animals' is a surreptitious or implicit way of confirming a certain interpretation of the human subject, which itself will have been the very lever of the worst violence carried out against nonhuman living beings," and explains Diamond's rejection of "rights philosophy . . . in thinking about our moral obligations to animals" by stressing that, for her, "the fundamental question of *justice* issues from an essentially different conceptual realm than the question of 'rights.'" Calarco, on the other hand, stresses that if continental thinkers like Martin Heidegger and Jacques Derrida approach ethics and the question of the animal outside the framework of rights it is not because their thinking is uncritically metaphysical or anthropocentric, but because they believe "that rights discourse and its axioms are themselves metaphysical," favorably referring to a text in which Derrida claims that the arguments of the authors engaged in animal liberation ethics are often badly articulated or philosophically inconsequential.

This is surprising. For if morality in the broad sense may leave room not only for the arbitrariness of specific worldviews but also for subtle discussions about the role of care, the sense of exposure, and the individual variation of attitudes, it is difficult not to agree with Joseph Raz, according to whom "on the plausible assumption that the only valid grounds on which the free pursuit by people of their own lives can be restricted are the needs, interests, and preferences of other people, it becomes plausible to regard (narrow) morality as rights-based."[16] After all, not only did human rights protect Jacques Derrida during his dangerous adventure, but also they protect most of us for most of our lives. Fundamental rights have been requested for discriminated-against ethnic groups, and are now requested for religiously and socially discriminated-against women. Fundamental rights, to borrow from Cora Diamond, may perhaps add to "the difficulties of philosophy," but they certainly subtract from "the difficulties of reality."

Against this framework, it is hard to understand the grounds for so easily dismissing rights. Hard, at least, unless one harbors the suspicion that what is at work here is the awareness that, while in the case of animals—already seen as the kinds of entities that can be subjected to an unconstrained cost-benefit aggregative calculus—the general theoretical rejection of "rights philosophy" can indeed have the effect of depriving them of the protective fence that rights erect around individuals, in the case of humans it can have no impact whatsoever on their actual moral treatment. And in fact, in situations in which the defense of "human rights" becomes a political requirement, it may happen that even Jacques Derrida goes so far as to claim that "We must more than ever stand on the side of human rights. We need human rights."[17] The overall (welcome?) result is that human rights can remain unaffected by the possible negative influence of the inclusion of other (nonhuman) beings in the universe of rights-bearers.

Can Emmanuel Levinas, the continental philosopher whose approach to ethics Matthew Calarco favors, overcome all these shortcomings? Can he offer a nonbiased and nonambiguous challenge to moral perfectionism and a solid foundation for an expanded ethical sphere? In order to deal with this questions, one should distinguish, as Calarco does, between Levinas's own views and the possibilities his approach implies.

As far as Levinas himself is concerned, double standards between humans and all the other entities are openly vindicated. If ethics can be seen as "an interruption of my egoism coming from the face of Other," Levinas is very clear that the Other is merely human. In the wake of the long-standing preoccupation in French philosophy with "man's" release (*arrachement*) from nature's bonds, he is convinced that humans are an entirely new phenomenon in relation to animals—that "the human breaks with pure being."[18] Accordingly, the face is not in its *purest* form in nonhuman beings—with no exception whatsoever, not even in the case of Bobby, the dog who, with his joyous greetings, gave him and his companions in the concentration camp some rare moments of happiness.[19] Actually, Levinas goes so far as to state, with a phrase that seems to contradict all his claims regarding the kind of "prereflective" consciousness involved in the moment when the subject is exposed, without any rational mediation, to the naked vulnerability of the Other's mute face, that he cannot say at what moment one has "the right to be called 'face.'"[20]

As Calarco aptly stresses, however, a Levinasian approach should not necessarily be confined to the kinds of ethical encounters Levinas himself emphasizes. In his challenging endeavor to contest the effort to determine "who does and does not belong to the moral community" (a point to which we shall return), Calarco aims at replacing what he sees as a logic of inclusion and exclusion with an alternative way of understanding ethics that, starting from Levinas's premises, can become rigorously and generously *agnostic*. What would this ethical perspective look like?

According to Calarco, the central issue concerning ethical agnosticism revolves around the kinds of entities that might call the moral agent into question—in other words, it concerns the limits of moral status. Such limits cannot be determined once and for all, but must remain unsettled. For "if it is indeed the case, as Levinas suggests, that ethics arises from an encounter with an Other who is fundamentally irreducible to and unanticipatable by my egoistic and cognitive machinations, and if it is indeed the case that we cannot know in advance where the face begins and ends, where moral status begins and ends, then we are obliged to proceed from the possibility that *anything* might take on a face." Then, being aware of the fact that such agnosticism can seem a *reductio ad absurdum*, Calarco counters the possible critics by asking whether a historical survey of the failures that attended the opposite attempt to draw *the* line is not enough to persuade us that this latter approach is inherently pernicious, both morally and politically.

Now, let's grant that an approach radically infected by perfectionism, such as that of Levinas—according to which nonhumans are inferior beings because, apart from not being able to attain universality on the theoretical level, they cannot reach universalization on the ethical level (that is, are not moral agents)[21]—can be sterilized, and that its formal structure can be differently employed. Let's also grant (but we shall come back to this) that, as John Coetzee seems to suggest in his defense of Calarco's views, in each of us there can take place something like a conversion experience centered on some other mute appeal of the kind that Levinas calls the look, in which "the existential autonomy of the Other" becomes irrefutable. There remains, however, a very serious problem.

Let us return for a moment to Levinas. Unlike Derrida, Levinas is very clear regarding his stance on rights—or, better, on *human* rights. Not only is he quoted as saying that "we need rights because we cannot have justice," but in an essay specifically devoted to the "rights of man (*sic*)" he defends, and hopes to see further extended, the rights to life, to security, and to "the equality of all men (*sic*) before the law."[22] Why does he do so, in spite of the fact that his theory is, like the one Calarco and Coetzee favor, essentially based on response and responsibility? That is, why *rights*? The answer mainly lies in the phrase just cited.

The conceptual linking of rights with the question of equality is frequent. Indeed, Ronald Dworkin, who has famously defended the idea that rights are "trumps" against both public and private claims, has argued that we need rights because they express an appeal to equality—because they have to do with treating individuals as equals, entitled to the same concern as others.[23] And, with the question of equality, we can go back to the point we temporarily set aside, that is, Calarco's criticism of the effort to determine "who does and does not belong to the moral community."

both in theory and in practice; and for most humans only "in practice." Is this fair to nonhumans? Or does it betray an inadvertent under-evaluation of their cognitive capacities? True, Coetzee also refers to "a life of reason," probably meaning a life *entirely* devoted to the exercise of reason; but he contrasts it with a life devoted to "brawling and guzzling and fucking," and appears to imply that this is what "animal life" amounts to.

Consider some examples. Plutarch already observed that animals are capable of syllogistic deduction, as seen in the case of the fox who is risking her life on a frozen lake: treading gently, she lays her ear to the ice to perceive the noise of the water, thereby reasoning that the ice is too thin. Imprisoned orangutans, on the other hand, if they notice an abandoned screwdriver, ignore it, lest a guard discover the oversight, then thoughtfully wait until night, when they finally proceed to use it to pick the locks or dismantle the cage and escape. When moats are dug to prevent them from breaking out of their "reserves," elephants patiently devote themselves to caving in the sides, carefully shoveling the earth with their tusks and turning the steep sides into gentle slopes to make the crossing easy. And dolphin parents or baboon leaders, after deciding that in some cases human beings may offer relevant help, can undertake the risk of being killed by staying for long past safety range to obtain an intervention in favor of their young, be they trapped in fishing line or lying sick in their deep hollow in the krans.[27]

What does all this show us? It shows that a view of animals that denies them a share in reason is an impoverished one—that animals reason very well, and, despite their lack of strictly Socratic skills, they can set aside their immediate passions and appetites in order to rationally devise solutions to important problems. And what do these examples have in common? The fact of showing that reason is a fundamental instrument in many life situations, especially in the most challenging ones, during which brawling and guzzling and fucking must be suspended. And just as human and nonhuman animals most often must reason to save themselves or their dear ones, so sometimes human animals have recourse to their peculiar reasoning tools to save other oppressed beings—that is, to redress injustice. Particularly in this case they *must* reason, as they must overcome obstacles, meet challenges, undermine ingrained attitudes and situations, fight adversaries. Moral progress has advanced through the arms of criticism at least as much as through the criticism of arms.

In this sense, the "rational mind"—which, by the way, may be seen as "part of the biological natural history of animals as are lactation . . . growth and digestion"[28]—can, and does, act in the interest and in the service of the "body." For what moral progress first saves are bodies. As Michel Foucault, a continental philosopher who devoted most of his work to the concrete analysis of power and power relationships, observed, the body is "directly involved in a political field; power relations have an immediate hold upon it; they invest it, mark it, train it, torture it, force it to carry out tasks, to perform ceremonies, to emit signs."[29] Oppressed bodies not only cannot devote themselves to an inhuman or godlike life—they cannot even enjoy any passions or appetites.

Therefore, even if we granted, for the sake of argument, that nonhuman animals do not reason, and that by devoting oneself to reasoning one shows oneself to have no animal life, this reasoning would still be worthy if devoted to the goal of liberating animals and their bodies, and of allowing them—or, for that matter, other human beings—to perform "the activities that allow them to live out their being-in-the-world most fully." Worthy indeed—and also necessary. For even if it may be difficult to make the world a better place merely through the use of reason— be it in the form of offering arguments or of envisaging new juridical frameworks—it is certainly more difficult to achieve this result by merely relying on the possibility that all members of our species are reached by "the appeal that might come at any moment in their lives." Though such an appeal might be a fundamental one for the moral agent, from the point of view of the moral patients it is too precarious a resource—especially in light of the human record in morality.

There still are double standards here. People were not "persuaded" that slaves, or women, should be enfranchised—most of them were compelled to alter their attitudes and habits. Not only are there human beings who know "the pleasure of stalking and slaying a beast less cunning and less strong than oneself, and cutting it up and cooking and eating it afterward," there are also human beings who have recently shown us how much they know the pleasure of raping and/or killing defenseless women from a different ethnic group. In the latter case, though unfortunately with insufficient decisiveness, we have appealed to a product of our own reasoning, the universal human rights doctrine, and we have tried to prevent them by force from pursuing such pleasure. Why should we in the case of animals wait until the last among human beings is "converted," supposing that this can ever happen? Why should we leave animal enfranchisement at the mercy of the casualness of human feelings? Are animals second-class beings (is our suffering worse than the cat's)? And if so, is it perhaps because of their allegedly *inferior cognitive skills?*

Distracting Difficulties

HARLAN B. MILLER

Science and Philosophy

It is easy to overstate the contrast between the analytic and the continental flavors of philosophy. The clumsiness of the distinction is apparent in the very labels, one by method and the other by geography. It is often a matter more of style than content, of family resemblances, as Calarco rightly says, with various hybrids and overlaps. Wittgenstein is usually put on the analytic side of the ledger, but he is surely as oracular and perplexing as any figure in the continentals list.

But there is one frequent difference that is noteworthy here: the view of the relation between philosophy and the empirical sciences. As a rule, analytic types see philosophy as continuous with the sciences. Philosophy is a colleague of science, a partner in the enterprise of constructing a unified and coherent picture of the universe and all its contents. The partnership is not an equal one, and only the old or old-fashioned of the analytic think philosophy the senior. In particular, what science (and ordinary observation) tells us about the world and about sentient beings is generally taken as clearly relevant to ethical discussion. In contrast, many continentals directly oppose, and not just rhetorically, philosophy and its enemy, science.

Cavalieri/Warnock overstates, I think, the independence of ethics from metaphysics. But she takes for granted the relevance of psychology. With the other friends of animals in the analytic tradition, she is quite happy to cite scientific evidence for nonhuman animal awareness. But this does not "derive ethical directives from empirical observations," as Wolfe fears. There is no violation of "Hume's Law" since, in addition to the empirical claims, there is an explicitly prescriptive premise: suffering is bad. There is already an "ought" in the premises as well as in the conclusion. The determination of moral status is finally scientific, in that science (in the broadest sense) tells us what sorts of things have morally relevant characteristics. But science does not tell us which characteristics are morally relevant. Of course, judgments of moral status are revisable, if we have come to doubt either the ethical or the empirical premises.

Ordinary Ethics

Wolfe quotes Kenneth Burke's claim that "virtues are by very definition rare and exceptional." Burke's definition is certainly not mine. (At least I hope so. It is possible, although surely unlikely, that his world is just much more evil than mine.) Perfect virtue is of course quite rare, as are perfect pitch and perfect pitching. Every day there are hundreds of thousands of demonstrations of honesty, kindness, self-sacrifice, truthfulness, and courage. There is plenty of vice too, of course, but that is no reason to deny that people again and again overcome their fears, help and protect both those they love and perfect strangers, tell the truth to their own disadvantage, and refrain from appropriating even what they covet. Most of this decent behavior is simply habitual. Aristotle's habituation has proved more efficacious, and much less intrusive, than Hobbes's Leviathan.

It is worth insisting on the ordinariness of virtuous action. I admire my neighbor's collection of ceramic turtles. In fact I covet it, and often think how I would like to possess the turtles. Perhaps I even fantasize about her giving them to me, or consider how much I could offer her to buy them. But it just doesn't occur to me to break into her house to steal them, or to falsify a will and contract to have her killed. It is not that I consider these things and reject them because of my fear of the law or of damnation, or my Kantian respect for the moral law. In fact, since I am at least partly a well brought-up adult, they just do not occur to me at all. They are her turtles, not mine. That's it.

Morality is not necessarily, or even commonly, a matter of challenges or interruptions of any sort, either in the style of Levinas or in Calarco's broader construal. As just noted, other people's possessions almost never "challenge" me with their attractiveness. I fairly often donate platelets, although I have never been challenged to do so and in fact have never (knowingly) met anyone who needed or received a platelet infusion. I abstain from eating meat in order not to contribute to non-human animal suffering. But the meat cases at the supermarket do not challenge me, and the animals from which their contents came are no longer able to do so.

Nor need concern for a hitherto neglected class of beings require any sort of conversion experience, *pace* Coetzee. Although I've met plenty of nonhuman animals, my conversion was essentially purely intellectual. I concluded, after several years, that the arguments of Peter Singer et al. were simply irresistible.[1] Much more important is the case of the rejection and eventual abolition of slavery in the Western world. Thousands and eventually millions of people became convinced that human slavery was an abomination. The position of a tiny minority in the ancient world became that of an overwhelming majority in Britain, France, and the northern parts of the United States. At this time (the late eighteenth and the first half of the nineteenth centuries) most of these people had never met a slave or had direct involvement with slavery. (Bristol and Boston partly suppressed their past and partly tried to atone for it.) Argument convinced these people, convinced many to the point of passion, without confrontation with the victims and often without any sort of conversion experience. (One of many differences between this case and that of the treatment of nonhumans is that almost everyone today *is* directly involved in the consumption and thus the suffering of nonhumans.)

Rights

Rights talk seems now to be inescapable in many contexts, especially "border" issues like abortion, vegetative states, and the treatment of nonhumans. But this talk, although almost necessary as rhetoric, is often confused, even more often confusing, and sometimes just muddled. A minor example: Wolfe refers to "the utilitarian calculus of animal rights philosopher Peter Singer." But the standard contrast in moral philosophy is between utilitarian calculations that weigh and balance competing interests, and ascriptions of rights, which exclude certain interests from any sort of calculation and hold them to be inviolable. Singer is in fact a utilitarian of a very sophisticated sort, with no absolute commitment to rights. He is an "animal rights philosopher" because he does occasionally use rights rhetoric.

Calarco characterizes rights discourse as metaphysical, and it often is, but this is, I believe, just misguided and the source of difficulties that are both insoluble and gratuitous.

Bentham, I believe, was both right and wrong on rights. He saw, correctly, that they are inventions, but he failed to see what beneficial inventions they are.[2] Rights are conventions of society (or government) that exempt certain sorts of activities and certain areas of behavior from being weighed in the balance. Rights are not natural objects, and we are not born with them as we are born with fingernails. They are wonderful inventions that are essential for human flourishing. They are created because the benefits of having certain things just out of bounds vastly outweigh the costs, either because of the security they provide for essential areas of life or because experience has shown the likelihood of self-deception, prejudice, and irremediable harm if we attempt to evaluate some sorts of action. Rights are declared, not discovered. Roman slaves did not have the right to be free. When we say that slavery violated their human rights, we are saying that they ought not to have been enslaved. This is a prescriptive, not a descriptive, claim. Declarations of rights, such as the UN Declaration of Universal Human Rights, are aspirational, not authoritative. I do not have an enforceable right to employment for the simple reason that no one has a duty to ensure that I have employment.

In Germany neo-Nazi speech is prohibited. In the United States it is considered protected (if obnoxious) speech. Which of these legal structures best corresponds with a natural human right to freedom of speech? Could that be decided by a committee of experts with intuitioscopes? Of course not, and legal provisions such as these are based, rightly, on empirically informed arguments about the balancing of interests. In this case, no one need suggest that human nature is different in these two countries. A defender of the German restrictions would instead refer to human history.

Mysticism about rights today derives partly from religion and, more significantly for our purposes, from Immanuel Kant. Kant, powerfully if differently influential in both analytic and continental thought, has cursed us all with what Wolfe rightly describes as the "fantasy of a noumenal self." This magical inhabitant of the kingdom of ends, in which we *must* believe, is inherently endowed with rights and especially with duties. But in fact there is no more reason to believe that you have (or rather are) such a self than to believe that your cat has (is) such a self.

Suppose I am just wrong about selves and rights. The main function of rights talk in the argument of Cavalieri's dialogue is quite independent of ontology. It just doesn't matter, in this context, whether rights are natural or artificial. This is the argument: if rights are to be ascribed to (or discovered in) all humans, it can only be on the basis of some morally relevant characteristics possessed by *all* humans. But the only such characteristics that can be found also characterize many nonhumans.

Distractions

To take nonhuman animals seriously as beings with interests is ipso facto to challenge a number of things that most of us just take for granted: meat on the table, hunting as recreation, leather shoes, etc. Some of the reactions to the discomfort this creates are ridiculous (denial that food animals are conscious; worries that surplus cattle will roam the land, trampling small children; insistence that vegetarianism is fatal). Much more sophisticated, and often more successful, are strategies that substitute avoidance for resistance. There are many flavors of what I will call "avoidance" talk, all of them effectively changing the subject from nonhuman interests to something else. As just noted, a concentration on the ontology of rights fits here, raising a cloud of bewilderment. If we think hard enough about rights, there's no time to think about hamburger.

Perhaps even more murky is the matter of the value of life. Is it better to live a wretched life than never to exist at all? Is the life of an infant more or less valuable than that of an adult? Why is the death of a young adult taken more seriously than the death of an old person? Do we really know that a human life is a more important thing than the life of a nonhuman?

Coetzee notes that the abstemious and intellectual lives of Cavalieri's characters are not available, or really accessible, to a horse or to his posited human who finds himself (doesn't seem to be herself) fully alive only when brawling, fucking, and/or guzzling. Of course, we very often can't get inside the head of others, human or nonhuman. Quite possibly we never can, and are only fooling ourselves when we think we are in perfect sympathy with another. A good novelist may give us the illusion that we are living the life, are inside the head, of a character, but it is, after all, both fictitious and illusory. It seems to me that I can get much closer to the life of the heroine of *Foe* than to that of Elizabeth Costello, even though the heroine's world is much further from mine than is Costello's.[3] There's no need to consider fiction. The world is full of humans whose minds I find opaque to the point of impossibility. What could it be like to be fascinated by Paris Hilton? Millions of religious fundamentalists (of several religions) actually believe things that I cannot even imagine believing. Their minds are just closed to me (and, doubtless, mine to theirs). Even though the lives of horses and members of the Taliban are in many ways opaque to me, I have no doubt that these creatures *have* lives, that they are capable of joy and suffering, and that that matters (at least in the case of the horses).

These are all fascinating matters, surely worth much discussion. But they should not be allow to distract us from the relatively straightforward topics of happiness and suffering. Despite these intellectual diversions, we still have to face our everyday choices.

Some, at least, in the continental tradition indulge in another kind of diversion. Derrida (as cited by Wolfe) laments the "industrial, scientific, technical violence" of animal agriculture, and Heidegger's criticisms of animal agriculture also focus on the technology.[4] It is not clear that this is moral criticism at all. Animal suffering is not even mentioned. Instead we get what I would call an aesthetic objection. For Heidegger, at least, it is clear that there could be no objection to traditional, postcard-village hands-on production of *pâté de fois gras*. Instead the objection is to technology and science displacing the genuine and truly human. The negative sense attached here to "scientific" brings us back to the start of this comment.

Postscript: Coetzee's Car

Coetzee proposes the unusable automobile he retains as metaphor for the slave species that depend on us. But the car to which he feels something like loyalty is an individual, not a species such as Volkswagen or Ford. The members of the slave species that provided our nourishment and gustatory delight are no longer around for us to protect. We can have no obligations to them. And if it is indeed sensible to talk about a duty to a species, there would not seem to be any obligation to maintain numbers as long as extinction is prevented. But it seems impossible that the species involved (chicken, turkey, cattle, sheep, swine) would become extinct. Some varieties ("breeds") might, but even those least well adapted to living on their own (e.g., Hereford cattle) would probably be maintained by fanciers. The first half of the twentieth century saw a drastic reduction, in fact a collapse, in the population of mules as they were replaced by trucks and tractors. The mule, of course, is a hybrid, not a species, and is sterile. But there are people who care about mules, enough people that muledom's future is safe at least for several more centuries.

On Appetite, the Right to Life, and Rational Ethics

JOHN M. COETZEE

(1) WHEN ONE is misunderstood it is usually because one has expressed oneself badly. So let me reiterate: there are human beings who, pushed into a corner, may be induced to say that it is the possession of reason that defines humanity, but who prefer not to be pushed into corners, and who at other moments in their lives, sometimes through words but far more often through their behavior, give expression to a conviction that we are most ourselves (meaning specifically that we as human beings are most ourselves) when we are living ourselves out most fully, or, as I earlier put it, are "brawling and guzzling and fucking" in our human way, just as "animals" (their way of putting it) are most themselves when they are doing the equivalent in their own animal way.

The more radical among such folk might even go on to say that to them what makes animal flesh better to eat than other food is precisely that another being has had to die in order for them to be fed: in effect, that by devouring not just the material residue of another being but the life of that being too, they are made more full of life themselves.

Philosophizing—it seems to me—is an activity unique in that it does not start out by demarcating its territory, putting bounds around itself. Thus it seems to me a legitimately philosophical problem how one is to confront an opponent who in some respects—e.g., where the satisfying of his/her human appetites is concerned—gives little or no weight to reasoning and the fruits of reasoning.

✧ ✧ ✧

(2) The question of rights. The paramount right is the right to life. In the case of domesticated animals, there is a twist to their right to life that is not always recognized. For the breeding of such animals, particularly livestock, is tightly controlled by the people who own them (own them body and soul). In practice this means that animals are called into being as dictated by the market (the market for their flesh). If tomorrow we approved and enforced a right to life for livestock, the immediate effect would be a moratorium on births as livestock owners cut back on no longer profitable herds. To put the case in an extreme form: a right to life for pigs means that within a few years the only pigs left on earth will be in zoos and sanctuaries.

I don't see why it should be a diversion (as Harlan Miller claims) to reflect on the consequences of pushing for a right to life in the absence of a right to multiply.

The right to life is usually taken to mean something like: if I am alive then I should not be deprived of my life. But in the case of livestock this interpretation is far too superficial. Which is better: not to be born at all, or to be born and then have one's throat cut in atrocious circumstances in early adolescence? Unimaginable though it may be, we should nevertheless try to imagine that choice being placed before each individual being—each, so to speak, pre-living individual being. I find it hard to imagine any one of us (whatever "us" may mean in this context) saying, "Better never to be born at all." It is the nature of life to live.

I am reminded of the image (Christian in origin, though no doubt heretical) of clouds of souls waiting to be born, calling on us (men and women) to bring them into the world by the only means known, incarnation. Who are we to deny these souls entry? (This may also be used as an argument against contraception, though I doubt that the mainstream Church would be prepared to use it.)

✧ ✧ ✧

(3) Regarding the project of a rational ethics, so thoroughly interrogated by Cary Wolfe, it is worth saying that there are people (among whom I number myself) who believe that our ethical impulses are prerational (I would be tempted to go along with Wordsworth and say that our birth is but a sleep and a forgetting, that what Wordsworth calls our moral being is more deeply founded within us than rationality itself), and that all that a rational ethics can achieve is to articulate and give form to ethical impulses.

Let me add that I by no means claim such an ethical foundation to the soul to be human and human alone. Many animals can clearly tell between just and unjust actions, at least as far as these directly affect them.

✧ ✧ ✧

(4) Regarding rights for nonhuman animals, enshrined in law, as a way of making the world a better place, let me simply put the question: if one actually wishes to bring about such rights, which is likely to be the more efficacious way of arguing for them: in the manner of the academic philosopher or in the manner of the parliamentary politician, that is to say, mixing true reasoning with verbal trickery, selective deployment of evidence, appeals to emotion, ad hominem attacks, and the denigration and browbeating of opponents?

"On a Certain Blindness in Human Beings"

CARY WOLFE

I'D LIKE TO begin with a joke, whose relevance to the current discussion will, I hope, become clear in due course:

A guy walks into his doctor's office one day and says, "Doc, I don't know exactly how to tell you this, but I'm *dead*. I know it sounds weird, and I really can't believe it myself, but I'm dead, I just know it."

The doctor replies, "C'mon, Bill, what do you mean you're *dead*? You're sitting here talking to me right now, aren't you? Don't be ridiculous. You're as alive as I am."

The patient shakes his head and responds, "I know it sounds crazy, and I don't understand it myself, but you have to believe me—I'm dead, I know it. Please believe me."

The doctor, understandably perplexed by what this longtime patient has just told him, sits back in his chair, rubs his chin for a while, and wonders what in the world he can prescribe for such an unusual and sensitive case. Finally, he hits upon a sure-fire remedy. He sits up in his chair, puts his hand on the patient's shoulder, and offers a solution.

"Okay, Bill, I have a way to treat your problem. For the next week, as you go about your daily business, I want you to repeat to yourself over and over, 'Dead men don't bleed, dead men don't bleed, dead men don't bleed.' Then come back and see me next Friday and we'll see where we are."

The patient is skeptical, but reluctantly agrees to give the treatment a try. As instructed, he repeats to himself over and over during the following week, "Dead men don't bleed, dead men don't bleed."

The following Friday, he returns to the doctor's office, as skeptical as ever. "I've done what you asked," he tells the doctor, "but I can't see that it has made any difference. I still feel the same way—I'm dead, I'm absolutely certain of it."

The doctor, undeterred, says to the patient, "Okay, Bill, hold out your hand." The patient does as instructed, and the doctor suddenly produces a needle from behind his back and pricks the patient's index finger, and a large drop of blood appears. "There, what do you think of *that*?" the doctor says triumphantly. And the patient, staring in amazement at his fingertip, looks up at the doctor and says, "Well, what do you know, Doc—dead men *do* bleed!"

✧ ✧ ✧

It would be easy to enter into a series of rebuttals, concessions, and refutations of some of the points raised in the responses to Cavalieri's dialogue. For example, it ought to be obvious that if you operate within the discourse of analytic philosophy, the differences between the work of Peter Singer's utilitarianism and Tom Regan's post-Kantian rights philosophy highlighted by Harlan Miller matter a lot; and if you operate outside that discourse, they don't matter much at all. From outside, what they have in common is far more important than what sets them apart, differences that are—for anyone *other* than an analytic philosopher—merely academic quibbles. They all theorize the morally relevant characteristics of subjectivity, whether human or nonhuman, on an anthropocentric model, in which the "interests" that are morally relevant (or the qualities that make one the "subject of a life," in Regan's more expanded sense) are possessed in greatest abundance by human beings. So continuing to point out that analytic philosophy misses the point about where its anthropocentrism is located *itself* misses the point, at this point, and there is really nowhere to go with this, since what analytic philosophy thinks constitutes its *anti*anthropocentrism is precisely what constitutes its *anthropocentrism* for "continental" philosophers. Is it worth running this circuit one more time? No.

This is not to say that I don't agree that perfectionism of the sort Cavalieri and Miller reject is inadequate to thinking about these questions—I clearly do, and I think everyone involved in this dialogue does.

This suggests to me that perfectionism of the traditional sort is a bit of a paper tiger. (I mean, even Martha Nussbaum has gotten on board the antiperfectionist wagon with her emphasis on "flourishing" and "capabilities" regardless of species in her recent book *Frontiers of Justice*, and she is about as big a fan of Rawlsian liberalism as you will find.[1]) So to me, rejecting traditional perfectionism is not the issue; the issue, as J. M. Coetzee and Matthew Calarco point out, is that Cavalieri's *way* of rejecting perfectionism is itself a kind of perfectionism.

Nor is this to say that using the existing juridical framework of rights is not (obviously) the most powerful way that we have at the moment of protecting nonhuman animals from maltreatment—it is. But the pragmatic expediency of the rights framework in liberal jurisprudence—which derives, after all, from a quite specific set of philosophical, historical, and ideological coordinates—does not in itself constitute an argument for the *philosophical* priority of the rights position (or the utilitarian one) at all. To suggest that it does, as Cavalieri does in her anecdote about Derrida's detention, is an utter non sequitur. This does not mean that the language of rights doesn't come in handy when you're trying to make political change—it is in fact indispensable, as any animal rights activist knows. But as Coetzee points out in the last paragraph of his second set of comments, all this means is that if you want to make changes in the law, you're going to have to use a large rhetorical toolbox to "turn" very different kinds of audiences (in the Mafia sense of the word) to your point of view. Philosophers don't change laws—shrewd rhetoric and political strategy (and money) do. Then, the question is just how concerned you want to be about the disjunction between the demands of the existing juridico-political framework and the philosophical position that motivates your desire to make change. That juncture, I suggest, is a specific pragmatic instance that will be handled differently by different people in different cases. But in no case, I think, will it have a linear or transparent or once-and-for-all relationship to the kinds of philosophical discussions we are having here.

I do, however, feel compelled (I am of the flesh, as Coetzee might say) to defend for a brief moment not myself but Derrida from what strike me as two rather egregious mischaracterizations. The first is Miller's assertion that Derrida's response to violence against animals is a merely "aesthetic objection." Even a cursory glance at Derrida's work on the animal question from *Of Spirit* forward makes clear that this is, to put it mildly, uncharitable. Derrida calls our treatment of animals in factory farming "violence that some would compare to the worst cases of genocide"—a comparison for which he (an Algerian Jew) took more than a little flack—and he declares the "suffering, pity and compassion" we must confront in the exposure of these conditions as fundamental to any ethical response. His focus on the *technology* of animal abuse, far from being a kind of Heideggerian pastoralism, is meant to draw attention to the issue that Coetzee rightly focuses on—an "infernal hell" for animals without end and without historical precedent because we now have, on a scale previously unknown, the ability to constantly supply this machinery of suffering and abuse with fresh bodies, new "lives" (if one can even call them that). There are numerous, equally pointed, and equally graphic invocations of the seriousness of animal suffering in Derrida's later work—too many to recount in the space I have here.

Similarly—and this is but an extension of the same mischaracterization—Cavalieri's reply attempts to collapse the distance between Derrida and Heidegger, as if Derrida's assertion of the "abyss" between *Homo sapiens* and other animals reproduces Heidegger's humanism. But Derrida explicitly calls Heidegger's assertion "dogmatic" because it is held in the face of a growing body of increasingly differentiated and specialized "zoological knowledge" that suggests otherwise, as Derrida is intent on reminding us.[2] The problem that Derrida has with Heidegger's resistance to "biological continuism" is not that it attends to the specificity of the human, but that it attends to the specificity of the human *only*, and thus reinstates the ontological divide between *Homo sapiens* and everything else. This is why he condemns "the strict enclosure of the definite article ('the Animal' and not 'animals')," which obscures the particularity and multiplicity—the *nongeneric* nature (vs. utilitarian "interests," for example)—of different kinds of living beings. And this particularity and multiplicity do not in any way correspond to the distinction "human/animal." The phrase "*the* Animal" doesn't just obscure the differences between humans and, say, geese; it *also* obscures "*the infinite space* that separates the lizard from the dog, the protozoon from the dolphin, the shark from the lamb, the parrot from the chimpanzee."[3] "Infinite space," I take it, is a synonym for "abyss," and it is an abyss that does not fall *between* the human and nonhuman animal but *among* different kinds of animals, human and nonhuman. So does Derrida think there is an "abyss" between most adult human beings and, say, a sparrow? Yes. He also thinks, however, that there is an abyss between a bonobo and a starfish, and I would agree with him. But because he is not arguing from the minimal standard of suffering invoked by Singer and admired by Cavalieri and Miller, and instead is speaking from a more broadly phenomenological perspective, Derrida's "abyss" ends up being rewritten by Cavalieri as a Heideggerian attempt to enforce the human/animal distinction. So who is really "in the grip of a theory" here?

When this sort of treatment is extended to Diamond—who quite obviously also takes the question of nonhuman suffering very seriously, harrowingly so, in fact—then the suggestion that begins to coalesce in Cavalieri's reply is that if you don't take nonhuman animal suffering seriously within the protocols and conventions of analytic philosophy, then you don't take it seriously at all. Period. "Ethics is too serious a matter to be subject to such maneuvers," Cavalieri writes of Derrida. But this conflates taking the question of our responsibilities to nonhuman animals seriously with hewing to the protocols of analytic philosophy. Again, an utter non sequitur.

Similarly, Cavalieri writes of Miller's sentence, "No attack on perfectionism can be simpler than 'You will not convince me that my suffering is worse than the cat's, nor in itself more important than the cat's.'" But what could be a more dogmatic assertion than "you *will not convince me*" of X? We know that—even within the narrow purview of analytic philosophy—Regan (in *The Case for Animal Rights*) rejects suffering alone as the basis for moral consideration, as does Nussbaum (just to name two). In fact, not even *Singer* agrees with the position so baldly formulated.[4] Who, then, is really engaging in "dogmatism and disdain for argument" here?

❖ ❖ ❖

What my little joke helps to illustrate is that to continue with a list of rebuttals, clarifications, and quibbles misses a quite fundamental and quite obvious point: that if philosophy as practiced and ethics as understood by Miller and Cavalieri is the antithesis of philosophy and ethics as practiced by, say, Derrida—and vice versa, of course (and both Miller and Calarco are right that the designation "continental philosophy" is of limited use here)—then what we are dealing with is not so much a case of disagreement as disconnection. Ships that pass in the night. People talking past each other. Is the way to proceed in the face of such intractability for one half of the philosophical universe to try to convince the other half that it has been wasting its time? I think not; otherwise, I would not have devoted hundreds of pages in my own work over the past twenty years to figures such as Singer, Regan, Rorty, Cavell, Nussbaum, and others not plausibly described as "continental."

One might think this nothing more than a thinly veiled apologia for philosophical "relativism," were it not for the fact that "relativism" itself is a bogus charge levied by those who think they have a corner on philosophical foundations. As Rorty puts it,

> The view that every tradition is as rational or as moral as every other could be held only by a god, someone who had no need to use (but only to mention) the terms "rational" or "moral," because she had no need to inquire or deliberate. Such a being would have escaped from history and conversation into contemplation and metanarrative. To accuse postmodernism of relativism is to try to put a metanarrative in the postmodernist's mouth.[5]

To encourage very different kinds of philosophy to cease recycling their fundamental differences on the terrain of ever smaller quibbles and to instead try to learn something from each other about what the vocation of philosophy can be, how it can be responsive to the suffering and exploitation of nonhuman animals that moves and engages thinkers across a range of approaches—this is not simply to promote a tepid "pluralism" either, which Niklas Luhmann rightly calls "the laziest of all compromises."[6] In fact, it is to give way to a more exacting demand, in which, I would suggest, *any* form of philosophy has to have built into it the inevitability and necessity of *other* points of view, *other* ways of thinking the problem (whatever that problem may be). As Luhmann would put it (though there is a Wittgensteinian version of this claim as well), the man in my little joke does not see, *and he cannot see that he does not see*. And this "not-seeing" is not something that can, in principle, be cured by argumentation, disabusing him of his false premises and unwarranted inferences. Indeed, this blindness is the very condition of possibility for seeing anything at all.

It might be useful, therefore, to find a way to reframe the stand-off between "analytic" and "continental" philosophy in other terms that might help disclose and explain their constitutive blindness to each other. There are several prominent versions of this view woven into the fabric of twentieth-century Western thought, but one of the more theoretically precise, I think, may be found in the later work of Niklas Luhmann, who, although a sociologist by training and trade, inherits and reworks many of the problems handled in phenomenology by Husserl and others. As Luhmann points out, observation ("seeing") changes fundamentally in the wake of modernity, and for quite identifiable historical and sociological reasons. For Luhmann, modernity (and with it "postmodernity") is a phenomenon of "functional differentiation," in which social interactions reach a threshold of complexity beyond which they are pragmatically better handled by discrete function systems (the education system, the legal system, the economic system, and so on) that carry out their observations by reducing complexity by means of a constitutive code (knowledge/ignorance, legal/illegal, profit/loss, etc.). In Luhmann's view (familiar to practiced readers of the early Foucault, among others), people don't communicate, discourses do (to use Foucault's phrasing), and they can only achieve any kind of effectivity *because* they are partial (in both senses of the word).

For Luhmann, then, all observations are contingent and selective constructions and reductions of an environment that cannot be grasped holistically or in any totalizing fashion. And what this means is that all observations are self-referential. This fact, however—what we might call in Hegelian parlance the "identity of difference" or "the identity of identity and nonidentity"—cannot be observed by the one who uses that distinction to carry out its operations. The legal system, for example, must remain "blind" to the paradoxical identity of the two opposite sides of its constitutive code "legal/illegal"—to the fact that both sides are in fact a product of only one side (namely the legal)—if it wants to use that code to maintain itself. *That* observation (the observation that, to put it slightly otherwise, the legal code is a self-instantiating tautology, "legal is legal") can only be made by *another* observer, a "second-order" observer, using a different code (in this case, education), which likewise must remain "blind" to the paradoxical nature of *its* constitutive distinction, which can only be disclosed by another observer, and so on and so forth.

Thus, as Luhmann summarizes it:

> The source of a distinction's guaranteeing reality lies in its own operative unity. It is, however, precisely as this unity that the distinction cannot be observed—except by means of another distinction which then assumes the function of a guarantor of reality. Another way of expressing this is to say the operation emerges simultaneously with the world which as a result remains cognitively unapproachable to the operation.
>
> The conclusion to be drawn from this is that the connection with the reality of the external world is established by the blind spot of the cognitive operation. Reality is what one does not perceive when one perceives it.[7]

"Reality," in other words, isn't occluded or obscured by difference; it is *produced* by difference. Observational self-reference and differentiation are not things to be overcome or surmounted; rather, "universalization can be achieved only through specification."[8]

The implications of all this for the idea of communication presumed by the dialogue form with which these discussions began are, I take it, obvious enough. The dialogue form—and the forms of subjectivity and intersubjectivity modeled by it—would amount to a fantasy that communication could be returned to its premodern conditions of transparency between subjects of "reflection" who have no unconscious (in either the Freudian, Marxian, Saussurian, or Lacanian senses); it presumes communication to be a face-to-face affair in which each party is, in principle, capable of seeing all, if only she be disabused of the distractions, bad ideas, false inferences, and so on that block her view.

This is not to say, of course, that the fantasy is impossible—it is possible just as a performance of Handel's *Messiah* is possible. It is simply to highlight the difference between the *form* of the dialogue and its *meaning*, how the function of that form, at this particular point in time, must be redescribed.

Indeed, Luhmann observes,

Already in the eighteenth century, a century of the incipient self-description of modern society, one finds a starting point for a very different style of observation, first in the novel. The novel enables the reader to observe something that the heroes of the novel—consider *Pamela*—*cannot* observe. Romanticism thereupon devises a style that relies upon the reader's *not* believing what the immediate description sets before him. With Marx, this technique of observation is transposed to social-scientific analysis. Marx sees through the delusive coherence of capitalism and makes this insight the basis of a critique of political economy. One need only mention Freud in order to recognize the breadth and explosive force of this way of observing.... Social class, therapist, free-floating intelligentsia—one continues to search for a position of observation that explains to oneself and to others their inability to see and that thereby places within reach knowledge of the world about which one can ultimately agree.[9]

Interestingly, Luhmann then mentions a little-known essay by William James, "On a Certain Blindness in Human Beings" (1899), published as part of a volume with the rather humble title, *Talks to Teachers on Psychology: And to Students on Some of Life's Ideals.* And it is to James I will now turn by way of conclusion—in part to make clear that I am not simply arguing for the priority of nonanalytic philosophy (James, as far as I know, has never been accused of practicing either "deconstruction" or "continental philosophy"), and in part because James's short essay helps bring us back to the question of what all this has to do with sharing life with our fellow creatures (and in this respect it helps to clarify the connection between the position I have been outlining in these remarks and what Calarco has in mind in his discussion of "agnostic ethics" at the end of his response).

James insists that we are, as "practical beings," profoundly isolated; we suffer from a "blindness with which we are all afflicted in regard to the feelings of creatures and people different from ourselves." Each of us is "bound to feel intensely the importance of his own duties," he writes, but "this feeling is in each of us a vital secret, for sympathy with which we vainly look to others." "The others," however, "are too much absorbed in their own vital secrets to take an interest in ours. Hence the stupidity and injustice of our opinions, so far as they deal with the significance of alien lives. Hence the falsity of our judgments, so far as they presume to decide in an absolute way on the value of other persons' conditions or ideals."[10]

For example, James continues in a wonderfully rendered passage,

> Take our dogs and ourselves, connected as we are by a tie more intimate than most ties in this world; and yet, outside of that tie of friendly fondness, how insensible, each of us, to all that makes life significant for the other!—we to the rapture of bones under hedges, or smells of trees and lamp-posts, they to the delights of literature and art. As you sit reading the most moving romance you ever fell upon, what sort of a judge is your fox-terrier of your behavior? With all his good will toward you, the nature of your conduct is absolutely excluded from his comprehension. To sit there like a senseless statue, when you might be taking him to walk and throwing sticks for him to catch! What queer disease is this that comes over you every day, of holding things and staring at them like that for hours together, paralyzed of motion and vacant of all conscious life? (267–68)

James's point is not that we fail to recognize the *same* life in others, but rather that we are so locked within our own form of life that we fail to recognize the myriad *other* forms of life around us—and so is the case for all "practical" creatures. "We are but finite," he continues, "and it seems as if energy in the service of [our] particular duties might be got only by hardening the heart toward everything unlike them" (272–73). "Only in some pitiful dreamer, . . . or when the common practical man becomes a lover, does the hard externality give way, and a gleam of insight into the ejective world . . . the world of inner life beyond us, so different from that of outer seeming, illuminate our mind. Then the whole scheme of our customary values gets confounded, then our self is riven and its narrow interests fly to pieces, then a new centre and a new perspective must be found" (273). In short, we are then taken out of ourselves, and not in recognition of others who are *like* ourselves, but of their "confounding" difference. Or rather—to be more exact about it—of others who *are* "like" us *only* insofar as they (like us) dwell in their self-referential difference, their mode of life.

What is the moral of these reflections, James asks at the end of his address:

> It absolutely forbids us to be forward in pronouncing on the meaning-lessness of forms of existence other than our own. . . . Hands off; neither the whole of truth nor the whole of good is revealed to any single observer, although each observer gains a partial superiority of insight from the peculiar position in which he stands. . . . It is enough to ask of each of us that he should be faithful to his own opportunities and make the most of his own blessings, without presuming to regulate the rest of the vast field. (285)

Is it enough? And does the compulsion to do more, to "regulate" in the name of a generic standard or ideal, thereby diminish the "vast field"? Those, it seems to me, are central questions for the discussions—and differences—that animate these pages.

Between Life and Rights

MATTHEW CALARCO

On Coetzee and Miller

John Coetzee's initial response to Cavalieri's dialogue suggests that her critique of perfectionism itself is an instance of performative perfectionism, inasmuch as it advocates for and grants a higher value to a life of reason that is closed to most human and nonhuman animals. A further problem, as Coetzee notes, is that individuals like Alexandra and Theo who live this kind of "bloodless" and "sexless" life apparently know nothing about "brawling and guzzling and fucking," any more than they know the pleasures of hunting and eating animal flesh. Thus, even though the "upper intelligentsia" might grant higher value to this life, there are other people (perhaps Coetzee himself) who think the upper intelligentsia are "missing the best of life."

The initial charge of performative perfectionism against Cavalieri strikes me as forced. Hierarchies pervade her work in both explicit and implicit ways, and I have tried to show how those hierarchies function in her texts in my initial response. But no hierarchy is to be found in the distinction she draws between a life of reason and one of pleasure. Cavalieri's thought consistently gives equal moral value to all forms of sentient, subjective life, no matter how little intellectually sophisticated they might be. That she privileges rational discourse in laying out her views on animal ethics need not entail that she is a perfectionist of any sort. Rational discourse could (and I would argue *should*) be seen here as but one tool at our disposal in rethinking and reorienting our practices in regard to animals. Further-more, if we follow Nietzsche[1] and view rational discourse as but one more drive in the service of other drives, as an emergent natural property belonging to a specific kind of animal with specific needs and limitations, then the life of reason becomes just one mode of life among many others. Not only will traces of it likely be found elsewhere among natural entities, it would certainly have no privileged place among those various ways of living, either from a naturalistic perspective or from the perspective of Cavalieri's work.

However, just as Nietzsche himself would argue,[2] Coetzee's "other folks" are no doubt correct that this near bloodless life of rational discourse misses "the best of life." And here is where I would agree with Coetzee's remarks and endorse his second claim that Cavalieri's discourse (and much of contemporary animal ethics) somehow fails to pay attention to and loses touch with pleasure, joy, violence, and *life* as such. At issue in animal ethics, for me at least, is nothing else but affirming life in this broad sense, which is to say, life understood as *irreparable* (to borrow a concept from Giorgio Agamben[3]). That life is linked to a certain amount of violence toward animals (and humans also, we should note) is an irreducible fact (and this should not be taken, of course, to imply that I *endorse* violence against animals). No animal ethics, no matter how pure and well-meaning, can overcome the irreducibility of violence. Now, it is unclear to me whether Cavalieri's vision of animal rights seeks to bring about an antiseptic world that is utterly without violence toward animals and other sentient beings; at the very least, she has little to say about such issues. But what is clear is that her ethical project of trying to challenge the dogmatically speciesist exploitation of animals *could* be seen as being on the side of life as such. What remains to be done is to illustrate in more detail exactly how her ethico-political project and the "best of life" can be joined together.

Harlan Miller's attempt to derive a conclusion similar to the one that Cavalieri draws about the moral status of animals *without* challenging human chauvinism and perfectionism shows just how ethically straightforward and undemanding it would be to extend basic moral consideration to animals. Miller, following Peter Singer, is surely right in maintaining that our daily practices often sacrifice the most vital and fundamental interests of animals for the most trivial and inconsequential interests of human beings.

When philosophers like Miller point out such matters to readers and challenge them to enact their moral principles in a more consistent manner, I have no real objection to offer. One could certainly lodge the same objections against Miller's argument that Coetzee raises in regard to Cavalieri's dialogue, and there is something to such charges when rational discourse becomes the *sine qua non* of animal ethics. But if Miller's argumentative strategy is reinscribed within a larger strategy and project that allows for a multiplicity of ways of writing about, thinking about, and reorienting our practices in regard to animals and our relations with them, I can subscribe to such arguments almost without reserve. Thus, rather than raising any objections to Miller, I would simply inquire about the intended *scope* of such argumentation. Are such philosophical arguments intended to suffice for transforming our interactions with animals, or does he see them as part of a larger project? Is becoming a vegetarian what is primarily at stake in doing and thinking about animal ethics? Do the ethical arguments Miller offers need to be supplemented by a larger critical analysis of the institutional, sociopolitical, and economic contexts in which we interact with animals? Can these contexts be transformed simply through ethical arguments, or do such arguments (as useful as they might be) need to be part of a much larger, more thoroughgoing transformational project? It is in view of these kinds of questions that the debates in animal ethics can be moved beyond the overly narrow focus on moral status and moral consideration and become truly transformational.

On Wolfe and Cavalieri

On the issues discussed in this exchange, my position is so close to Wolfe's as to be indistinguishable. There are areas where our respective projects diverge, primarily at the level of politics and strategy, but to explain those divergences in a manner that would do justice to his position would take us well beyond the scope of this volume. Here I will simply register my agreement with his thesis that Cavalieri's thought, while avowedly and fundamentally antispeciesist, remains humanist, which is to say metaphysical and reliant upon a problematic and exclusionary notion of subjectivity.

Cavalieri views the critique of humanism and rights discourse that Wolfe and I (along with Derrida and other posthumanist thinkers) employ as being "dismissive" of rights and the moral and political advances they have helped to achieve. I will not try to speak for Wolfe here, but I suggest that this kind of critical analysis is not intended to be dismissive of such advances. On the contrary, at least in my case, I am critical and suspicious of rights discourse not because of its progressive potential (which I endorse) but because it is *inherently* perfectionist. Theories of moral rights are always founded on the idea of an inside and an outside, of members and nonmembers, and so forth. Cavalieri's notion of moral rights, as developed in her dialogue and in such books as *The Animal Question*, is no exception. Her theory is built on the explicit exclusion of all nonsubject entities from the realm of moral concern, and it is *this* exclusion that is at the heart of my objection to her work. I am fully in support of eliminating perfectionism from ethics, but I want to apply that standard in a more radical and thorough manner than she does in her account of animal ethics. The notion of universal moral consideration that I am putting forward is fundamentally opposed to any and all perfectionism and certainly does *not* imply that certain beings should have lesser or inferior rights to those of human beings.

What rights discourse effectively does when applied to animals or any other marginalized being or group is challenge existing moral hierarchies, and that is something I fully endorse. But rights discourse makes these advances while simultaneously promoting new hierarchies and new exclusions—and the task of ethical philosophy as I see it is to challenge such hierarchies and imagine alternative ways to think about ethics that are decidedly nonhierarchical, nonperfectionist, and nonexclusionary. All of us agree that the major aim of animal ethics should be to challenge dominant ways of thinking about and relating to animals. The chief question is whether this important project will proceed via a new set of exclusions that are just as pernicious and dogmatic as the exclusions it seeks to overcome.

Notes

Foreword

1. See, for example, Richard A. Posner, *The Problematics of Moral and Legal Theory* (Cambridge, Mass.: Harvard University Press, 1999).
2. See James Jasper and Dorothy Nelkin, *The Animal Rights Crusade: The Growth of a Moral Protest* (New York: Free Press, 1992) in which they write, "Philosophers served as midwives of the animal rights movement in the late 1970s" (90).

The Death of the Animal: A Dialogue on Perfectionism

1. Stephen Toulmin, *The Place of Reason in Ethics* (Cambridge: Cambridge University Press, 1950), 131–32.
2. On this see Florence Burgat, *Animal, mon prochain* (Paris: Editions Odile Jacob, 1997), 17.
3. Emmanuel Levinas, *Difficult Freedom*, trans. Seàn Hand (Baltimore: Johns Hopkins University Press, 1990), 153. See on this Peter Atterton, "Ethical Cynicism," in *Animal Philosophy: Essential Readings in Continental Thought*, ed. Matthew Calarco and Peter Atterton (New York: Continuum, 2004), 51–61.
4. Raymond Corbey, *The Metaphysics of Apes: Negotiating the Animal-Human Boundary* (Cambridge: Cambridge University Press, 2005), 112, 185, and passim.
5. *Genesis* I: 28.
6. Friedrich Nietzsche, *Human, All-Too-Human*, Part I, trans. Helen Zimmern (London: Allen & Unwin, 1909), §110.
7. Martin Heidegger, *An Introduction to Metaphysics*, trans. Ralph Mannheim (New Haven and London: Yale University Press, 1987), 1.

8. Martin Heidegger, "Letter on Humanism," in *Basic Writings, Revised and Expanded Edition,* ed. David Farrell Krell (San Francisco: Harper, 1993), 235.

9. Ibid., 217.

10. David Hume, *A Treatise of Human Nature* (Oxford: Clarendon Press, 1978), 469.

11. Aldo Leopold, *A Sand County Almanac* (Oxford: Oxford University Press, 1949), 224–25.

12. Rudolph Carnap, "The Elimination of Metaphysics Through Logical Analysis of Language," in *Logical Positivism,* ed. A. J. Ayer (Glencoe, Ill.: The Free Press, 1959), 80.

13. Arthur Schopenhauer, *The World as Will and Representation* (New York: Dover, 1969); Arthur Schopenhauer, *On the Basis of Morality,* trans. E. F. J. Payne (Indianapolis: Bobbs-Merrill, 1965).

14. Arthur Schopenhauer, "On Women," in *Arthur Schopenhauer: Essays and Aphorisms,* trans. R. J. Hollingdale (London: Penguin, 1970).

15. Peter F. Strawson, "Social Morality and Individual Ideal," *Philosophy: The Journal of the Royal Institute of Philosophy* 36 (Jan. 1968): 1–17; Geoffrey J. Warnock, *The Object of Morality* (London: Methuen, 1971), 148.

16. Aristotle, *Politics,* Book I, 2.

17. Thomas Aquinas, *Summa Theologica* I q. 92 a. 1; ibid., II–II q. 70 a. 3.

18. Mary Midgley, *Animals and Why They Matter* (Athens: University of Georgia Press, 1983), ch. 7.

19. Martin Heidegger, *The Fundamental Concepts of Metaphysics: World, Finitude, Solitude,* trans. W. McNeill and N. Walker (Bloomington: Indiana University Press, 1995), 177.

20. See Friedrich Nietzsche, *Beyond Good and Evil,* trans. W. Kaufmann (New York: Vintage, 1989) and in more detail in Friedrich Nietzsche, *On the Genealogy of Morals,* trans. W. Kaufmann (New York: Vintage, 1969).

21. Jerome B. Schneewind, "The Misfortunes of Virtue," in *Virtue Ethics,* ed. Roger Crisp and Michael Slote (Oxford: Oxford University Press, 1997), 200, 179.

22. Immanuel Kant, "Theory and Practice," in *Kant's Political Writings,* ed. H. Reiss, trans. H. B. Nisbet, 2nd ed. (Cambridge: Cambridge University Press, 1991), 74 ff.

23. Porphyry, *On Abstinence from Animal Food,* Book III, 2 and 19. See on this Daniel A. Dombrowski, "Vegetarianism and the Argument from Marginal Cases in Porphyry," *Journal of the History of Ideas* 45 (1984): 141–43.

24. For the notion of "object" see Warnock, *The Object of Morality.* For the notion of "function" see Toulmin, *The Place of Reason in Ethics,* ch. 10.

25. Kant, "Theory and Practice," 79.

26. John Rawls, *A Theory of Justice* (Oxford: Oxford University Press, 1971), 136 ff.

27. James Rachels, *Created from Animals: The Moral Implications of Darwinism* (Oxford: Oxford University Press, 1990), 190–93.

28. Edward Johnson, *Species and Morality*, Ph.D. diss., Princeton University, July 1976 [Ann Arbor, MI: University Microfilms International, 1977], 134.

29. Schopenhauer, *On the Basis of Morality*, 91.

30. Nietzsche, *Human, All-Too-Human*, aphorism 92.

31. David Hume, *An Inquiry Concerning the Principles of Morals* (Indianapolis: Hackett, 1983), Sect. III, Part I.

32. Brian Barry, *Theories of Justice* (Berkeley: University of California Press, 1989), 163.

33. Cf. Alfred J. Ayer, *Language, Truth and Logic* (1935; reprint, New York: Dover, 1952), and Charles L. Stevenson, *Ethics and Language* (1944; reprint, New Haven and London: Yale University Press, 1960).

34. Ludwig Wittgenstein, "A Lecture on Ethics," ed. Rush Rhees, *Philosophical Review* 74 (1965): 8.

35. Ben Bradley, "Two Conceptions of Intrinsic Value," paper presented at the First Annual Bellingham Summer Philosophy Conference, Western Washington University, August 5–7, 2000, http://web.syr.edu/~wbradley/2IV.htm#_edn1.

36. G. E. Moore, *Principia Ethica* (Cambridge: Cambridge University Press, 1993), ch. I, C, 15 and ff.

37. Immanuel Kant, *Groundwork of the Metaphysics of Morals*, trans. Mary Gregor (Cambridge: Cambridge University Press, 1997), 37.

38. Immanuel Kant, *Lectures on Ethics*, trans. Louis Infield (New York: Harper and Row, 1963), 148–54.

39. David DeGrazia, *Taking Animals Seriously* (Cambridge: Cambridge University Press, 1996), 250.

40. See, e.g., Raymond G. Frey, "Autonomy and the Value of Animal Life," *The Monist* 70 (1987): 50–63.

41. See, e.g., Michael Tooley, "Abortion and Infanticide," *Philosophy & Public Affairs* 2 (1972): 37–65.

42. Cf., e.g., Tom Regan, *The Case for Animal Rights* (Berkeley: University of California Press, 1983), 324–25.

43. E.g., Jacques Derrida, "Force of Law: The 'Mystical Foundation of Authority,'" trans. Mary Quaintance, in *Deconstruction and the Possibility of Justice*, ed. Drucilla Cornell, Michael Rosenfeld, and David Gray Carlson (London: Routledge, 1992), 24.

44. See on this Paola Cavalieri, *The Animal Question* (New York: Oxford University Press, 2001), 112–13.

45. Cf. Peter Singer, *Practical Ethics* (Cambridge: Cambridge University Press, 1979), 89–90. On this, see Cavalieri, *The Animal Question*, 109–11.

46. Heidegger, *The Fundamental Concepts of Metaphysics*, 196–9.

47. See Irenaus Eibl-Eibesfeldt, *Ethology: The Biology of Behavior*, 2nd ed. (New York: Holt, Rinehart and Winston, 1975), XV, 2, B, c), 3.

48. E.g., Henry Friedlander. *The Origins of Nazi Genocide: From Euthanasia to the Final Solution* (Chapel Hill and London: North Carolina University Press, 1995); Mary V. Seeman, "Psychiatry in the Nazi Era," *The Canadian Journal of Psychiatry* 50, no. 4 (March 2005): 218–25.

49. Peter Singer, *Animal Liberation*, 2nd ed. (New York: New York Review of Books, 1990), 6 and passim.

50. E.g., Henry Sidgwick, *The Methods of Ethics*, 7th ed. (Indianapolis: Hackett, 1907), 79.

51. Peter Singer, *The Expanding Circle: Ethics and Sociobiology* (New York: Farrar, Straus & Giroux, 1981), 88.

Humanist and Posthumanist Antispeciesism

1. Kenneth Burke, *Counter-Statement* (1931; reprint, Berkeley: University of California Press, 1968), 120, 114.

2. Jacques Derrida, "The Animal That Therefore I Am (More to Follow)," trans. David Wills, *Critical Inquiry* 28 (Winter 2002): 399–400, 394–95. See Coetzee's short article, "Exposing the Beast: Factory Farming Must Be Called to the Slaughterhouse," *Sydney Morning Herald*, February 22, 2007, http://www.smh.com.au/articles/2007/02/21/1171733846249.html. Further references to Derrida's essay are given in the text.

3. A relevant and related passage on this point may be found in Cavalieri's *The Animal Question*, trans. Catherine Woollard (Oxford: Oxford University Press, 2001), 139: "on the basis of the very doctrine that establishes them, human rights are not *human*. On the one hand, the more or less avowed acceptance of the idea that species membership is not morally relevant has de facto eliminated from the best foundation of the theory any structural reference to the possession of a genotype *Homo sapiens*. And, on the other, the will to secure equal fundamental rights to all human beings, including the non-paradigmatic ones, has implied that the characteristics appealed to in order to justify the ascription of such rights could no longer be those (seen as) typically human but should instead lie at a cognitive-emotive level accessible to a large number of nonhuman animals. In this sense, not only is there nothing in the doctrine of human rights to motivate the reference to our species present in the phrase but it is the same justificatory argument underlying it that drives us toward the attribution of human rights to members of species other than our own." It is not clear to me how "not *human*" here can mean anything *other than* empirically derived (i.e., "cognitive-emotive level accessible to a large number of nonhuman animals"). It is pre-

cisely this problem, of course, that motivates Heidegger's *ontological* investigation, which, despite its problems (well noted by Derrida), is set against the "biological continuism" whose most "sinister" aspects include racism, the use of naturalism to countenance xenophobia, and much else besides. All of which is very much to the point, of course, in understanding Heidegger's complex relationship to Nazism. See Derrida's *Of Spirit: Heidegger and the Question*, trans. Geoffrey Bennington and Rachel Bowlby (Chicago: University of Chicago Press, 1989), 56.

4. Stanley Cavell, *Conditions Handsome and Unhandsome: The Constitution of Emersonian Perfectionism* (Chicago: University of Chicago Press, 1990), xxiii. Further references are in the text.

5. J. M. Coetzee, *The Lives of Animals,* ed. and intro. by Amy Gutman (Princeton: Princeton University Press, 1999), 43.

6. Cora Diamond, "The Difficulty of Reality and the Difficulty of Philosophy," in Stanley Cavell, Cora Diamond, John McDowell, Ian Hacking, and Cary Wolfe, *Philosophy and Animal Life* (New York: Columbia University Press, 2008), 45–46. Further references are in the text.

7. Cora Diamond, "Injustice and Animals," in *Slow Cures and Bad Philosophers: Essays on Wittgenstein, Medicine, and Bioethics*, ed. Carl Elliott (Durham, N.C.: Duke University Press, 2001), 121. Further references are in the text.

8. "Losing Your Concepts," *Ethics* 98, no. 2 (January 1998): 276.

9. "Experimenting on Animals: A Problem in Ethics," in Cora Diamond, *The Realistic Spirit: Wittgenstein, Philosophy, and the Mind* (Cambridge, Mass.: MIT Press, 1991), 350. Further references are given in the text.

10. Jacques Derrida, "Force of Law: The 'Mystical Foundation of Authority,'" trans. Mary Quaintance, in *Deconstruction and the Possibility of Justice*, ed. Drucilla Cornell, Michael Rosenfeld, and David Gray Carlson (London: Routledge, 1992), 24. Further references are given in the text.

11. Jacques Derrida, "Afterword: Toward an Ethic of Discusson," in *Limited Inc.*, trans. Samuel Weber et al., ed. Gerald Graff (Evanston, Ill.: Northwestern University Press, 1988), 116, 148.

12. "Violence Against Animals," in Jacques Derrida and Elisabeth Roudinesco, *For What Tomorrow . . . : A Dialogue*, trans. Jeff Fort (Stanford: Stanford University Press, 2004), 63. Further references are in the text.

13. Jacques Derrida, "'Eating Well,' or The Calculation of the Subject: An Interview with Jacques Derrida," in *Who Comes After the Subject?*, ed. Eduardo Cadava, Peter Connor, and Jean-Luc Nancy (New York: Routledge, 1991), 116–17.

14. Here is Derrida again: "to confer or to recognize rights for 'animals' is a surreptitious or implicit way of confirming a certain interpretation of the human subject, which itself will have been the very lever of the worst violence carried out against nonhuman living beings" ("Violence Against Animals" 65).

No Escape

1. For a recent restatement of a radically dichotomous view cf. Peter Carruthers, "Natural Theories of Consciousness," *European Journal of Philosophy* 2 (1998), http://psyche.cs.monash.edu.au/v4/psyche-4-03-carruthers.html. For a response, see Paola Cavalieri and Harlan B. Miller, "Automata, Receptacles, and Selves," *Psyche* 5, no. 24 (1999), http://psyche.cs.monash.edu.au/v5/psyche-5-24-cavalieri.html.
2. René Descartes, *Discourse on the Method and Meditations on First Philosophy*, ed. David Weissman (New Haven and London: Yale University Press, 1996), 35–36.
3. Cf. for example: Irene Pepperberg, *The Alex Studies: Cognitive and Communicative Abilities of Grey Parrots* (Cambridge, Mass.: Harvard University Press, 1999); Thomas I. White, *In Defense of Dolphins: The New Moral Frontier* (Oxford: Blackwell, 2007); and Sue Savage-Rumbaugh, Stuart G. Shanker, and Talbot J. Taylor, *Apes, Language, and the Human Mind* (New York: Oxford University Press, 1998).
4. See John Rawls, *A Theory of Justice* (Oxford: Oxford University Press, 1973), 504–5, 128.
5. On this cf., e.g., John Robbin, *The Food Revolution: How Your Diet Can Help Save Your Life and Our World* (San Francisco, Calif: Conari Press, 2000).

Toward an Agnostic Animal Ethics

1. In addition to her dialogue presented in this volume, I shall refer to the following writings by Paola Cavalieri: *The Animal Question*, trans. Catherine Woollard (New York: Oxford University Press, 2001); "Are Human Rights Human?," *Logos* 4, no. 2 (2005), http://www.logosjournal.com/issue_4.2/cavalieri.htm (accessed May 1, 2007); "The Animal Debate: A Reexamination," in *In Defense of Animals*, ed. Peter Singer (Malden, Mass.: Blackwell, 2006), 54–68; and "Animals and the Limits of Justice," *Logos* 5, no. 3 (2006), http://www.logosjournal.com/issue_5.3/cavalieri.htm (accessed April 30, 2007).
2. See, for example, Tom Regan's discussion of perfectionism in *The Case for Animal Rights* (Berkeley: University of California Press, 1983), 233–35. It should be noted that Cavalieri's critique of perfectionism is considerably more demanding and rigorous than Regan's.
3. See Baruch A. Brody, "Defending Animal Research: An International Perspective," in *Why Animal Experimentation Matters: The Use of Animals in Medical Research*, ed. Ellen Frankel Paul and Jeffrey Paul (New Brunswick, N.J.: Transaction, 2001).

4. See Cavalieri, *The Animal Question*, 27; "Are Human Rights *Human*?"; and "Animals and the Limits of Justice."
5. Cavalieri, *The Animal Question*, 25.
6. Cavalieri, "The Animal Debate," 63.
7. To take but one example, Emmanuel Levinas explicitly argues throughout all of his work that ethics precedes, and should serve to ground, theoretical and metaphysical reflection.
8. Derrida takes up this issue at length in an interview with Elisabeth Roudinesco, "Violence Against Animals," in Jacques Derrida and Elisabeth Roudinesco, *For What Tomorrow?*, trans. Jeff Fort (Stanford: Stanford University Press, 2004).
9. See page 3 of this volume.
10. Cavalieri, *The Animal Question*, 27.
11. Ibid., v.
12. I should mention that a number of feminist and ecofeminist philosophers (for example, Karen Warren, Greta Gaard, and Carol Adams) make this same point with considerable force.
13. Thomas Birch, "Moral Considerability and Universal Consideration," *Environmental Ethics* 15 (1993): 313–32.
14. Ibid., 321.
15. Ibid., 315.
16. Ibid., 328.
17. See Jacques Derrida, *L'animal que donc je suis*, ed. Marie-Louise Mallett (Paris: Galiée, 2006).
18. For the classic feminist version of this approach, see Carol Adams, *The Sexual Politics of Meat: A Feminist-Vegetarian Critical Theory* (New York: Continuum, 1990). For a socialist and sociological version, see David Nibert, *Animal Rights/Human Rights: Entanglements of Oppression and Liberation* (Lanham, Md.: Rowman and Littlefield, 2002).

Pushing Things Forward

1. Giorgio Colli, *La nascita della filosofia* (Milan: Adelphi, 1975).
2. See, e.g., Hans Georg Gadamer, "On the Possibility of a Philosophical Ethics," in H. G. Gadamer, *Hermeneutics, Religion and Ethics*, trans. Joel Weinsheimer (New Haven: Yale University Press, 2000).
3. Riccardo Giacconi, "L'universo senza motore," *Il sole 24 ore*, June 24, 2007.
4. Friedrich Nietzsche, Letter to Mathilde Maier, July 1878; www.geocities.com\thenietzschechannel\nlett1878.htm.
5. Cf. Geoffrey J. Warnock, *English Philosophy Since 1900*, 2nd ed. (Oxford: Oxford University Press, 1969), 42.

6. Serge Lellouche, "La critique du totalitarisme et le déclin du marxisme," *Sciences Humaines*, http://www.scienceshumaines.com/index.php?lg=fr&id_article=12234.

7. Jacques Derrida, "The Animal That Therefore I Am (More to Follow)," trans. David Wills, *Critical Inquiry* 28, no. 2 (2002): 394–95; and Jacques Derrida (with Jean-Luc Nancy), "'Eating Well,' or the Calculation of the Subject: An Interview with Jacques Derrida," in *Who Comes After the Subject*, ed. Eduardo Cadava et al. (New York: Routledge, 1991), 112.

8. Derrida (with Nancy), "'Eating Well,'" 115. See also Jacques Derrida and Elisabeth Roudinesco, *De quoi demain . . . Dialogue* (Paris: Fayard/Galilée, 2001), 113–14.

9. Derrida and Roudinesco, *De quoi demain*, 113–14. For the comment on the use of "asinine" cf. David L. Clark, "On Being 'the Last Kantian in Nazi Germany': Dwelling with Animals After Levinas," in *Animal Acts: Configuring the Human in Western History*, ed. Jennifer Ham and Matthew Senior (New York and London: Routledge, 1997), 188. For the abyssal rupture see, e.g., Derrida, "The Animal That Therefore I Am," 398–99, and Derrida and Roudinesco, *De quoi demain*, 112, 121.

10. Jacques Derrida, *De l'esprit. Heidegger et la question* (Paris: Editions Galilée, 1987), 64.

11. Stanley Cavell, "Companionable Thinking," in *Wittgenstein and the Moral Life*, ed. Alice Crary (Cambridge, Mass.: MIT Press, 2007), 296 ff.

12. Cora Diamond, "Experimenting on Animals: A Problem in Ethics," in *The Realistic Spirit* (Cambridge, Mass.: MIT Press, 1995), 351.

13. Stephen R.L. Clark, "The Absence of a Gap Between Facts and Values, II," *Proceedings of the Aristotelian Society*, Suppl. vol. 54 (1980): 236.

14. Richard Wasserstrom, "Rights, Human Rights, and Racial Discrimination," in *Moral Problems*, 3rd ed., ed. James Rachels (New York: Harper & Row, 1979), 11.

15. Jeremy Waldron, ed., *Theories of Rights* (Oxford: Oxford University Press, 1984), Introduction, 5.

16. Joseph Raz, "Right-Based Moralities," in ibid., 198.

17. Jacques Derrida, "Autoimmunity: Real and Symbolic Suicides—A Dialogue with Jacques Derrida," in *Philosophy in a Time of Terror: Dialogues with Jurgen Habermas and Jacques Derrida*, ed. Giovanna Borradori (Chicago: University of Chicago Press, 2003), 132–33.

18. Emmanuel Levinas, "The Paradox of Morality," trans. Andrew Benjamin and Tamra Wright, in *The Provocation of Levinas: Rethinking the Other*, ed. Robert Bernasconi and David Wood (London and New York: Routledge, 1988), 172.

19. On Bobby see Emmanuel Levinas, "The Name of a Dog, or Natural Rights," in *Difficult Freedom: Essays on Judaism*, trans. Seán Hand (Baltimore: Johns Hopkins University Press, 1990), 151–53. Cf. on this Paola Cavalieri, "A Missed Opportunity: Humanism, Anti-humanism and the Animal Question," in *An-*

imal Subjects: An Ethical Reader in a Posthuman World, ed. Jodey Castricano (Waterloo: Wilfrid Laurier University Press, 2008).

20. Levinas, "The Paradox of Morality," 169.

21. Cf., e.g., Emmanuel Levinas, "Language and Proximity," in *Collected Philosophical Writings*, trans. Alphonso Lingis (The Hague and Boston: Martinus Nijhoff, 1987), 122; Emmanuel Levinas, *Totality and Infinity: An Essay on Exteriority*, trans. Alphonso Lingis (Pittsburgh: Duquesne University Press, 1969), II:D.

22. Emmanuel Levinas, "The Rights of Man and the Rights of the Other Man," in *Outside the Subject* (Stanford: Stanford University Press, 1993), 120–21.

23. Ronald Dworkin, "Rights as Trumps," in Waldron, ed., *Theories of Rights*, 153–67; and Ronald Dworkin, *Taking Rights Seriously* (Cambridge, Mass.: Harvard University Press, 1977), esp. 91–92 and 184–205.

24. Levinas, "The Paradox of Morality," 170.

25. Mary Midgley, *Animals and Why They Matter* (Athens: University of Georgia Press, 1983), 99.

26. Cf. Marie-Angèle Hermitte, "Le droits de l'homme pour les humains, les droits du singe pour les grands singes!", *Le Débat* 108 (January–February 2000): 168–74.

27. See: Plutarch, *De Sollertia Animalium*, 13; H. Lyn White Miles, "Language and the Orang-utan: The Old 'Person' of the Forest," in *The Great Ape Project: Equality Beyond Humanity*, ed. Paola Cavalieri and Peter Singer (New York: St. Martin's Press, 1994), 45; Joyce H. Poole, "An Exploration of a Commonality Between Ourselves and Elephants," *Etica & Animali* 9 (1998): 96; Jamal Thalji, "A Leap of Faith, Gratitude," *St. Petersburg Times*, March 13, 2007; and Eugene N. Marais, *My Friends the Baboons* (London: Blond and Briggs, 1975), 118 ff.

28. John Searle, "Animal Minds," *Etica & Animali* 9 (1998): 37–50.

29. Michel Foucault, *Discipline and Punish: The Birth of the Prison* (New York: Vintage, 1995), 25–26.

Distracting Difficulties

1. See at least Peter Singer, *Animal Liberation*, 2nd ed. (New York: New York Review of Books, 1990).

2. Remember his famous claim that natural rights are "simple nonsense"; see Jeremy Bentham, "Anarchical Fallacies," in *Nonsense Upon Stilts*, ed. Jeremy Waldron (London: Methuen, 1987), 53.

3. See J. M. Coetzee, *Foe* (London: Secker & Warburg, 1986); and J. M. Coetzee, *The Lives of Animals*, ed. and intro. by Amy Gutmann (Princeton: Princeton University Press, 2000).

4. Martin Heidegger, text of a conference held in Bremen in 1949, quoted in